THE KGB'S  MOST WANTED

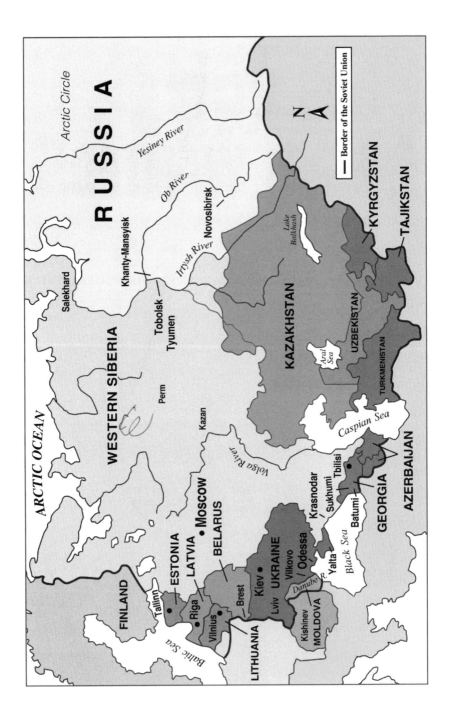

THE KGB'S
MOST WANTED

THE STORY OF JOSEPH BONDARENKO, RUSSIAN EVANGELIST

JOSEPH BONDARENKO

credo
house publishers

Grand Rapids • Michigan

Published by Credo House Publishers,
a division of Credo Communications, LLC, Grand Rapids, Michigan.
www.credohousepublishers.com

ISBN: 978-1-625860-11-8

Scripture quotations taken from the New American Standard Bible®,
Copyright © 1960, 1962, 1963, 1968, 1971, 1972, 1973, 1975, 1977, 1995
by The Lockman Foundation
Used by permission. (www.Lockman.org)

Photo section and map by Vitaly Manzuk
Cover and interior design by Sharon VanLoozenoord
Edited by Grace and Truth Communications LLC

Printed in the United States of America
First edition

To my beloved wife Maria,
my dear children Lidia, Vera, Daniel,
Anna, Mariam and their families,
with love and gratitude.

❈ ❈ ❈

"I thank God for the story of your life and I consider it to be my honor to have been your co-worker on Christ's field in those historic days in Moscow."

BILLY GRAHAM

Contents

Acknowledgments

FIRST AND FOREMOST, I AM GRATEFUL to my marvelous God and Creator for giving me life and guiding the course of my path; for loving and calling me to partake in His kingdom-building here on earth; for helping me and guiding my thoughts in the process of writing this book; for the eternal hope of rejoicing in the works of His hands, His brilliant mind, and creative power of the Spirit.

I am indebted to my wife, Maria, for faithfully standing beside me throughout the years and being my pure joy and inspiration. She is a detailed and meticulous person whom God used mightily in the course of my life and ministry, especially in bringing about this book. Without her dedication, valuable input, and thoughts, it wouldn't be the same.

I would like to thank all of my wonderful children for their blessing and vital presence in my life. To Daniel and Yana, Peter and Lidia, Timothy and Anna for all the help, prayerful and financial support, resources and encouragement they have given me throughout these years; especially to my daughter Vera and her husband, Dennis, for devoting their time and efforts toward this book; for her writing, translating, editing, overseeing, and managing this project from beginning till end. Her wholehearted commitment, diligence, patience, and ability to put thoughts into words were indispensable in making this book a reality. To my son-in-law Vitaly and daughter Mariam for their enthusiasm and heart, committing the time and professional skills into the preparation of the materials, patiently going through the high volume of pictures and documents, and organizing photographs. I have experienced even more love of my family during this lengthy process.

No words can express my heartfelt gratitude to Ronald and Suzanne Brewer, who were among the first in California to befriend us. Their example of Christian living and proven love in words and actions, and like-mindedness radiated Christ's light into our challenging days in a new country. Ronald's initial translation of the manuscript and supportiveness helped bring my story to life. Ronald permanently changed his address to the heavenly Jerusalem and won't read this book. His early departure to a heavenly home causes us heartache to this day, but his legacy and good works live on in our hearts.

I am indebted to my faithful friends Charles and Dotty Duke, who urged and inspired me to write. Their true friendship, excellent support, prayers, and insights served a great deal of encouragement to my family and me.

My deep appreciation goes to writer Lorilee Craker, a *New York Times* bestselling author whose father was born in Ukraine, and who enthusiastically stood up to the challenge of crafting my manuscript and reshaping the story with American readers in mind. Her writing experience, skills, background, and knowledge of the history, time, and culture involved gave it a richer flavor and brought it to its best.

I also thank my good friend Dr. Valery Zhakevich for his prayers, timely advice, and healthy criticism that improved the manuscript.

The Rev. Ben Patterson, Campus Pastor at Westmont College and a dear member of our church family, has been enormously generous and wise as he advised us about just the right publishing solution for the English edition of the book.

I am thankful to our publisher, Tim Beals of Credo House Publishers, for his professional assistance in guiding us through the complicated and time-consuming publishing process. His critique, constructive suggestions, and recommendations were invaluable for preparing the book for publication. Thanks also to Paul Brinkerhoff, who edited the manuscript so carefully and thoroughly, making important corrections and contributions along the way.

I wish to acknowledge Eugenia Semenovna Ginzburg and to the input provided by her autobiography, *Journey into the Whirlwind*, translated by Paul Stevenson and Max Hayward (1967; repr., New York: Harcourt Brace Jovanovich, 1975). Some of the descriptions I offer of what I experienced of persecution, especially in Soviet prisons, are similar in nature to those given in Mrs. Ginzburg's memoirs. The reasons she and I and others were persecuted may differ, but the stories we tell about our experiences often sound similar because they are shared in common by those who somehow survived and lived to tell about it.

Lastly, my sincere heartfelt gratitude goes to the many friends and acquaintances who genuinely encouraged, supported, continually prayed, and assisted in different areas and details; also to those who have been with me in my trials and blessings, who shared my passion for evangelism and my love for God and people. As I continue to press on, this resounding truth echoes in my heart: there is no greater joy in life than to serve the purposes of God and persevere to do what we are called to do despite the circumstances.

Preface

IT'S NATURAL FOR A PERSON who has walked most of his life's journey to look back, on the sorrows and pleasures of the past and at the people who have had an effect on you, for good and evil.

My destiny hasn't been easy to fulfill. I was born and lived most of my life in an atheistic country that confessed and promoted the religion of violence and cruelty. I was born an enemy of the godless authorities. From my earliest days I was hated for my faith, as were all who sincerely believed in God.

I want to share the story of my life, not because I consider it to be special, but to tell you, my reader, of the Lord's deeds and the blessings His children enjoy even when going through "the valley of the shadow of the death."

God's ways are inscrutable and holy. He leads us on our way, often not only to believe in Him, but also to suffer for His sake. These memories are a testimony to Jesus' closeness to each of us, whether we are persecuted and enslaved or we are being tested by freedom. It is so important to live according to His commandments, to be able to forgive and bless one's persecutors and pray for those who offend you.

I feel especially called to share my story with young people, who may not ever face the kinds of trials and sufferings born by their parents and grandparents.

I hope when you are reading my story, some of you will be able to "extract the precious from the worthless" (Jer. 15:19). Some will gain some counsel, and some will understand their spiritual search in a new way. Others may look at their lives and decide to make changes, to become more firm in faith, and to find their way serving God and people.

It took me a long time to decide to write this book. My family urged me to write it, as did many friends around the world, including my dear friend the American astronaut Charles Duke.

Time was passing by. For a long while I couldn't make up my mind to start. But as my seventieth birthday approached, God inspired me to start describing my path. The final nudge was a letter from my former cellmate, Pavel, with whom I had shared the Good News while in prison and for whom I had been praying for many years. The seeds planted in those unbelievably rough conditions bore fruit, and Pavel was serving the Lord! If my experiences could help point one man to the light, perhaps they could point others as well.

A note: As I was not able to keep a diary, and most of my papers and notes were confiscated by the KGB, my story is based mainly on memory. Fortunately, I have a good memory!

My prayer is that this book would become a blessing for each of my readers, a life-giving spring of encouragement for their souls in difficult times. May your faith in God be increased and work wonders in your life, in that of your family, your local church, and beyond.

Prologue

The Prosecutor's Office

"But the LORD was with Joseph and extended
kindness to him, and gave him favor."

GENESIS 39:21

WHEN I WALKED ALONG the crowded Deribasovskaya Street in
Odessa, Ukraine, on my way to the prosecutor's office that day in
1962, I remember how the sun shone on my young, strong back as I
gripped a subpoena in my hands. Had I known what was to come,
I would have been terrified; as it was, I felt surprisingly calm, although my thoughts became a bit more anxious as my steps grew
closer to the office.

That I felt calm at all was a miracle. The KGB (*Komitet gosudarst-
vennoĭ bezopasnosti* or Committee for State Security) was the chief
intelligence agency for the Soviet Union. They were the government's secret police and had eyes everywhere. They were very powerful and much feared by the people, and not without reason. Just
one month beforehand, I had been summoned to the KGB office,
where I was interrogated and beaten badly by two officers. Yet I
had been allowed to leave, and was still free as I walked down the
street.

The truth was, I didn't know what would happen behind closed doors in that office. Would I be beaten again? Could this be the day I would be imprisoned? Dilapidated buildings with overgrown shrubs, bushy grass, and tangled weeds lined my path as I walked toward this uncertainty.

I was twenty-six years old, with my whole life ahead of me. Little did I know I would soon lose the innocence of my youth.

Intently looking at the faces of people passing me, I tried to guess what they were thinking. What were their troubles and their plans? But all of them were in such a hurry. Quickly, they passed by me with indifferent faces. Like me, they also had unfinished plans.

Filled with these thoughts, I passed by the Opera Theater and entered the building of the regional prosecutor's office on Pushkin Street. My feeling of anxiety grew as an overworked official filled in my admission papers, marking the time of my arrival. He left the column blank indicating the time I would leave. For a moment, this gave me a glimpse of hope. *When I'm done here, they'll just fill in that column with a time, and I will leave this dank office, and go back to a life of freedom.*

Important-looking officials with a certain swagger strutted with purpose along the corridors. I was told to report to Room 28, and I passed a series of closed doors on my way there. Pausing for a few seconds at the appointed door, I knocked.

The official inside grabbed a sheet of paper. Writing with big block letters I could clearly see, he wrote "THE PROTOCOL OF INTER-ROGATION—BONDARENKO." His eyes were angry and dark as he proceeded to shout accusations and questions at me without giving me a chance to reply.

Finally, the interrogator opened his safe and placed a gun on the table before me. "Don't even think about escape," he said, in a voice studded with malice. "Don't you understand? You are under arrest. You are not a witness, but an incarcerated individual. You are a criminal. Right now, you will be taken to the KPZ [a preliminary imprisonment cell]."

❈ ❈ ❈

Someone once said to me that when you are arrested, it is like jumping down into an abyss. It's better by far to jump down without looking back at the beautiful world you are leaving behind, possibly forever.

A prison guard dressed in military garb shouted to a nearby officer, "Search him and arrange all the papers!" They searched me thoroughly. Then, they undressed me, removing even the laces from my shoes. Their fingers were like snails, slow and slippery as they also searched my body. Finally, the search was over. The most important proof of my crime—my Bible—was confiscated. "Now, go to your cell," one of the guards barked. "You sit there until you confess your guilt and give up your faith in your God."

I spent five days in that preliminary imprisonment cell. I don't know why, but I felt neither dejection nor despair, only an odd but certain joy. All I wanted to do was sleep, even though the only place to do so was the clammy concrete floor. So I slept and slept, twisting my body into a fetal position.

On the fifth day I was called to see the investigator. "How was your night?" he asked sarcastically.

"Thank you," I replied calmly. "I slept well, better than ever. There is only one problem. It is too damp and cold in there."

Confused, the investigator grew belligerent. "If you do not *behave* properly, and if you are stubborn, we shall beat out of you that good sleep!" He glared at me as he ranted. "Give up your delirious religious notions. Become a normal Soviet and enjoy freedom. It's up to you. Otherwise, you will have plenty of time to get familiar with prison life."

A KGB representative was present at the interrogation. He was the author of all the questions, and he directed the course of the interrogation. "Take him to his cell!" he ordered with a wave of his hand. "There he will have more time to think about everything. Then, we shall see if he will continue to be brave and courageous."

The unfriendly meeting was over. In a *voronok*, a car especially equipped for transporting criminals, I was driven to the prison.

Upon arrival at the prison, I was in for a rude awakening. I tried to appear calm, yet inside I was shocked at what I saw. My solitary cell, dark and frigid, was in the basement of the prison. There was nothing in the room except a *parasha* (a rusty iron pot used as a toilet). I could see that there was no bed and I would have to sleep on the cold, concrete floor. The instant the guards left I felt terribly lonely. Numbness and chill sank into my body.

There were swarms of questions. What had I done wrong? Why was I here? Maybe I was too outspoken, brave, or naïve. Did I really accomplish what the church entrusted to me? Maybe I had gone way beyond the call of duty, speaking so boldly about my faith while others kept silent.

Lord! Don't be silent. Please, answer my questions. Scatter the doubts that overcome my soul.

My prayers came fast and furious. I don't know how long I was praying, but suddenly a calm assurance and even a kind of joy filled my heart. I sat up and started singing, even though it felt strange to sing in that tomb-like cell. "Count your blessings, name them one by one; Count your blessings; see what God hath done . . ."

Comforting images and good, sweet memories began to filter into my mind and soul. Like a slideshow, I could picture snapshots of my whole life thus far, beginning with my childhood.

1

Born Under the Lucky Christmas Star

THEY TELL ME IT WAS A QUIET, starry night on December 15, 1936, when I was born, the ninth child of the bustling and friendly Bondarenko family. It took my family a long time to decide what to call me. Father gathered all the children together and told them his suggestion: Joseph.

My siblings did not like Joseph. They wanted their new brother to be called Victor or Anatoly or their favorite, Yevgeny. "Let's cast lots," Father suggested. "Bring me some paper and a hat. Each of you will write your favorite name on a piece of paper. Whatever piece of paper I shall pick from the hat will be his name."

Nadya and Sasha, my older sisters, set an additional condition: "We will agree to call him Joseph only if that name is selected three times. Otherwise, we will not babysit your Joseph!"

Each of them wrote a name on a piece of paper, rolled it up and threw it into the hat. My father plucked the first piece of paper out of the hat. "Joseph," he said, eyes twinkling.

"Again, again!" my brothers and sisters cried out.

The second piece of paper pulled from the hat also said "Joseph."

"Let Dad be blindfolded," one of the children said. "Then we will know for sure he's being honest."

When the third piece of paper was unfolded, it was so quiet you could hear a fly buzzing around the room. My father took off his blindfold and read the name, which of course was also "Joseph."

There were no more objections. All conditions had been met. My father liked the name Joseph, but moreover he admired the Bible character whose dramatic story had a happy ending. God gave Joseph such steadfastness that no ferocious winds or trials could slow him down. Maybe Father wanted Joseph's strength to rub off on me, his namesake.

According to my mother (whose voice was full of pain as she recounted this), when I was ten months old, I scalded myself with boiling water and received serious burns. My older sister Nadya was taking care of me when some guests came to our home and passed out presents for each of us. There had been a samovar (an urn with a spigot used to heat and serve tea) on the table, and in all the excitement, she didn't notice me grabbing it and turning it over on myself.

Nadya remembers how badly she felt. "I didn't care about the guests anymore," she recalls. "I was crying so bitterly, not because I was afraid of the punishment from my parents, but because of my brother's loud screams. I was feeling so sorry for him, and I was blaming myself for my carelessness. But there was no time for tears. We had to do something to help him. We grated potatoes and placed the gruel on the burnt spots. That seemed to give him some relief."

After my sister applied the poultice of potatoes, my parents took me to the hospital, where I stayed for two months to be treated for my burns.

My Remarkable Parents

My parents were born and reared in the Ukrainian village of Kapitanovka, hidden among the forests and fields of the Kirovograd region more than two hundred miles north of the large seaport city of Odessa on the Black Sea coast. Though my father, Daniel, was born to a peasant's family, he managed to arrange a wedding to my mother, despite his poverty. They were married in 1917, the same year all of Russia exploded because of the Russian Revolution, which actually was a series of revolutions and upheavals that ultimately paved the way for the formation of the Union of Soviet Socialist Republics (USSR).

In the October Revolution, the Bolshevik party, led by Vladimir Lenin, and the workers' Soviets, overthrew the Provisional Government in Saint Petersburg. The Bolsheviks appointed themselves as leaders of various government ministries and seized control of the countryside, establishing the Cheka to quash dissent. To end Russia's participation in the First World War, the Bolshevik leaders signed the Treaty of Brest-Litovsk with Germany in March 1918.

Civil war erupted between the "Red" (Bolshevik), and "White" (anti-Bolshevik) factions, which was to continue for several years, with the Bolsheviks ultimately victorious. While many notable historical events occurred in Moscow and Saint Petersburg, there was also a visible movement in cities throughout the state, among national minorities throughout the empire and in the rural areas, where peasants took over and redistributed land.

Everything was in ruins, and anarchy replaced order and discipline. People seemed to have lost their minds, behaving like crazy people with no laws.

During this time, my father needed money to buy some property so he and my mother could have a decent home together. A few of his friends approached him about joining them to go to a nearby village and rob a certain rich widow.

"Daniel, come on, join us," they coaxed. "It will cost you nothing to help us. You will just stand alongside observing."

"What is it that you are conspiring? I don't want to take a risk," my father said.

"What risk are you talking about?"

"I know such deals do not end well."

They did not give up easily.

"Come on! We will divide the spoils among ourselves. You will get some too! You'll see. You will be satisfied."

But my father didn't agree. He would not join their dangerous escapade. He listened to the voice of his conscience and stayed at home. The friends went without him. Soon enough, my father learned that his friends had killed the widow when she refused to give them her valuables. His friends had become killers.

Later, these young men were caught and taken to the village council. One of them managed to get free and escaped. He ran for thirty yards or so before he saw a well, which he dove into head first. People rushed to try and save him, but it was too late. He was dead.

His mother had said previously that she would rather see her son lying in a coffin than see him become a *Stundist* (originally a term of reproach derived from the German word *Stunde*, "hour," referring to a believer who meets together with other believers for reading the Scriptures and prayer, usually for an hour, a practice perceived as forsaking the Orthodox Church). Her words turned out to be prophetic. She saw her son's death take place before her own eyes.

Another of the killers fell prey to an angry mob. The crowd tore him to pieces on the village square. This story became a major turning point for my father. As he reflected on what had caused him to make the right choice while his friends had made the wrong one, he realized he had been influenced by a missionary he had met some time before his friends' fatal plot.

After this episode, my father and his friend Varpholomey Dovgenko started attending the *Stundist* meetings. With Ivan Dovgenko, one of the Evangelical believers living in Kapitanovka, conducting the services, only fourteen people were yet in the group. My father made an important decision, asking God for two things: to forgive him his past sinful life and to bless his new life in Jesus Christ. Both he and his friend joined the church and his new life began.

Still, he had many hurdles to overcome, as it was extremely difficult in the days of the Bolsheviks to live as an openly Christian person. Even his wife, my mother, was upset about him becoming a man of faith.

My mother, Zinaida Bondarenko, was born as well to a poor peasant's family and was a devout Orthodox Christian believer. Her mother, Felonida, hoped her daughter would marry a man from a large family, and my grandmother got her wish. My father's family already included eight members.

As a newlywed, my mother knew that her husband was attending the Evangelical believer's meetings, but she was sure he was not serious. When he told her that he had become a believer, she was scared. She worried how people in their village would treat him. She would cry, prevailing upon him not to abandon their "ancestor's faith."

"Don't cry," he had said to her. "Come with me, see the church I attend."

Her crying turned into sobbing. "Oh, Daniel, our life is good for nothing! You have become a *Stundist*! What shall we do?"

Grandmother Felonida was a prudent lady, and at that crucial moment she offered my mother the right advice: "Do as the proverb says: 'The thread follows the needle.' Unity within the family is a sure guarantee for happiness and prosperity." During Easter 1921, my mother took Felonida's advice. She joined my father at the meeting, where she heard the message of God's love for her. She responded by getting on her knees, confessing her sins, and turning her life over Christ. Their journey would not be easy, but they were traveling the same narrow path, reconciled to each other and their God.

They were very poor, but eventually my parents acquired some property, on which they built a small house and a shed. Afterward, they purchased a cow. Mother, the daughter of peasants, was thrilled to be the owner of her own property. But this prosperity did not last long. Soon trouble came, in various forms.

One night, during a thunderstorm, lightning struck the house and immediately burst into flames. My parents, who were sleeping, awoke and were deafened by the thunderbolt. Stunned, at first they could not move even a finger, although they knew they must run and save their lives. A cat and her kittens that were sleeping under the bed were killed in an instant. Fire spread everywhere.

Father grabbed my mother and their two-year-old son, my brother Boris, and raced to the neighbors. All the villagers came to gaze at the blaze. Some of the people were trying to extinguish the flames, but all was in vain. The house continued burning. In spite of a heavy rainstorm, everything was completely burned to the ground. My parents became homeless. The village people were supportive and compassionate, helping by bringing clothes and money to the fire victims. They even assisted the young family in building a new, tiny little house. It was a new beginning, but little did they know the tribulations that were just beginning.

You see, as time passed, my father continued to irritate the local authorities. They knew he believed in and had ceased to participate actively in USSR-approved public life. So they began to threaten him, promising they would destroy his house and throw him in a prison unless he changed his ways. In prison, they said, he would be forced to repudiate his God. But he paid no attention to their threats and their warnings, leveled at him via interrogations by the Village Soviet (a local judicial council). He continued to share his faith; surely, he could not repudiate the One who was more precious than life to him.

Plain folk in the village liked my dad, for he was friendly and helpful to all who met him. After a four-year program, he graduated from parochial school and was literate according to the standards of that time. He assisted many people in the village by arranging their documents and writing letters for them, and he was a skilled tailor who made clothes for the whole neighborhood. In my memory, I can see my dad walking down the streets of his native village Kapitanovka, taking off his cap and greeting everyone he met. The fellow villagers respected his kindness and honesty.

Father's hobby was beekeeping, which gave his soul much pleasure. He became experienced and skillful as a beekeeper. He gave honey to his neighbors, especially to the poor and the sick. When his household grew large, he started working at a station as a forest ranger. As payment, he received firewood to heat his house. Half the wood he received for the year he gave away to those in need. There were times when he gave away all he had, for he knew that others needed it more than his own family. But God, seeing his sacrifice, never left our family in need. This example of generosity, as well as our father's love for God and people, became a beautiful living lesson for us, his children, for the rest of our lives.

My mother also left a deep impression on my life. After a hard day's work, I remember her sitting by a burning thin stick (used instead of a candle), reading her Bible. From her childhood, she learned to love work, and industriousness was a quality she respected in everyone.

Love and discipline combined to shape her character. Mother had an uncanny ability to endure suffering for the sake of her children. Backbreaking labor and adversities of life would eventually undermine her health. In my mind's eye, I always picture her bent almost to the ground, busily working in the kitchen or in the vegetable garden, with a blessed smile on her face. Together, with my father, she sowed seeds of faith in us all.

Famine and Persecution

One of the great adversities my parents faced was the well-known Soviet famine of 1932–33 known as Holodomor. In their village, people were starving and entire families were dying. During that horrible time, my family survived only by God's mercy.

Later, my father was elected to lead the church in our village. He was a pastor for more than forty years. The members of the church loved him for his simplicity, sincerity, and his shepherd-like care for each one of them.

Obviously, it was extremely difficult to lead a church during this time, for the Soviet powers persecuted many believers. Many of the ministers were exiled to Siberia. The Orthodox Church in our village

was destroyed. Sincere believers were put on various trials, often
to defend themselves against trumped-up accusations. The writer
L. Kovalenko described that period in Russian church history as ut-
ter chaos and horror. The Soviets battled the kulaks (wealthy land-
owners) at the same level of intensity as they persecuted regular
folks and especially Christians. The public knew about how the Soviets targeted the kulaks and exiled them to Siberia, but they didn't
know how bad it was for the rest of us. According to Kovalenko, the
Soviets would arrange for "entire families, including babies and the
elderly, from the villages and farms of Ukraine and Belarus . . . to
be exiled to the Far North regions, dooming them to certain death."

My family escaped this fate but lived through the "Great Terror"
with grace and faith. My humble parents were like a kind of fifth
"Gospel" for me and the other children to read daily. Their example
of grace under fire gave me strength in my own life, during the dark
and difficult days that were to come.

2

A Childhood in the USSR

THERE WERE TEN CHILDREN in our family: Boris, Mary, Vladimir, Nadezhda (Nadya), Vasily, Alexandra (Sasha), Paul, Peter, myself, and Anatoly. My mother used to say, "One is not less than the other." My parents, brothers, and sisters were my true friends, and as a rule, we spent most of our free time at home. We even played together in a family string orchestra. Our parents taught us to love, respect, and take care of each other.

In 1939, the Soviets forced the idea of a kolkhoz, or a collective farm, on us. This meant no individual or family owned their own property anymore; it was all to be shared with everyone else. They took away our vegetable garden and our big orchard. We now had no right to pick a single apple from the orchard that originally belonged to us. Our mother was forced to go and work in the kolkhoz.

During one cold, chilly day in autumn, she took me with her to work on the farm, and I fell sick and could hardly breathe. Thankfully, there was a doctor named Anna who lived in our village. She was a kind and supportive woman with a wonderful soul. She quickly examined me and determined I was choking to death from an abscess in my throat. "There is no time to bring your little boy to the hospital," she said to my mother. "You must agree that I shall operate on him myself. If the blockage is removed, he will remain alive." My mother could see I was gasping for air and getting worse, so she agreed.

The doctor wiped her finger with some alcohol and pierced the abscess inside my throat with her own finger, freeing up my air passageway and saving my life.

Before the collective farm took away our garden, I remember when we children would go to the railway station to sell pears, apples, and plums grown in our orchard to passengers on the trains. (Thankfully, years later when I was a schoolboy my family was able to use their garden again.)

We had to rush at breakneck speed just to catch the passing train because it would only stop momentarily. Sometimes, people took our buckets into the compartments, and when the train began to move would throw the buckets back with no money to pay for the fruit. We were naturally very upset by the injustice of this, but my mother was calm and tried to reason with us. "At least they gave the buckets back," she said, since buckets were scarce during that time. "Try to do good, even when people treat you unfairly." The child who earned the most money received a prize, such as a bike trip to the nearby village or a fishing trip.

Work abounded for each of us. We were taught to work from our earliest years. We worked in the vegetable garden, the orchard, and the house. We collected bundles of firewood from the forest, herded the cows, and even assisted dad in his tailoring. He hand retailored worn-out things and made them look brand new.

Winters in our region were extremely cold. Sometimes, the snow would accumulate up to the smokestack, and it was only possible to leave the house through a tunnel dug in the snow. Our dad would take us outside to run in the snow, barefoot and semi-dressed. The frost burned our bodies, but we were so enthusiastic. This was Dad's method of getting us used to cold weather. After five minutes of exercise, we hurried into the house and warmed ourselves on the *petch* (a Russian chimney stove with a sleeping ledge). Together, we would read the Scriptures and listen to Bible stories, and afterward, we would sing songs accompanied by the balalaika (a Russian triangular wooden instrument that resembled a guitar) and the mandolin.

Near the house was a pond, and in winter we would ice-skate and play a type of ice hockey on its shiny surface. After arriving back home, wet and exhausted, we would have our family supper, everyone eating out of one pot. "Don't dare yawn!" a Russian saying goes. "If you don't fetch fast, there may be nothing to eat."

As spring arrived, we needed to earn our living. So we went to the kolkhoz to weed the gardens of sugar beets and corn sprouts. The beds were about a hundred yards long; but as evening approached, they seemed like a whole kilometer. It was hard work. Salty sweat poured into our eyes as we worked to achieve our quotas. The working rate equaled a *trudaden* (wages for one day of work paid in grain or sugar, not money). After work, despite being quite exhausted, we would run into the forest to play hide-and-seek.

In the summer we arose with the dawn. After breakfast, together with the neighbor's children, we took the cows to graze in the forest or in the field. We loved to walk barefoot on the cool, dewy grass.

In the fall we picked mushrooms, berries, and forest nuts. You could drink as much water as you desired from the rippling stream. As I sat down on a stump, I could hear the squeaking of trees, the rustling of the leaves, or even observe the ants and their industrious life. It is not possible to forget such a childhood spent in one's own family home!

War and School

In the summer of 1941, World War II descended on our country, filling people's hearts with fear and dread. Two regimes and two ideologies that despised each other faced off in a deadly battle. Who would survive?

The front line blasted through the village of Kapitanovka;

missiles were exploding and people perished. People hated the war, for all it brought was death and grief. Our unbelieving neighbors hid in cellars with us, and we all earnestly repeated together "God be with us!"

The war confiscated the best years of my childhood, but by 1945 the bloodshed was over and it was safe to return to school. I eagerly wanted to learn how to read and write. There were no workbooks, and we had to use pieces of newspaper instead. Since my family could not afford shoes for everyone, we thought about attending on alternate days. But none of us wanted to miss our lessons, so we willingly ran to school barefoot, bouncing on feet that were turning blue because of the morning frost.

For the first time in my life, I faced an overtly hostile attitude because of my religious upbringing. My siblings and I were often insulted. Teachers lowered our grades and banished us from certain lessons. They disgraced us by making us stand up at school meetings. "*Stundists*," they jeered. Atheist school officials even threatened to take us from our parents.

We were considered second-rate children, deprived of a wonderful Soviet future and a deserved place within the Communist society. They tried to force us to join the Komsomol (Communist Union of Youth), but we refused.

The headmaster, a devout Communist, hated us most of all. I still remember his name: Grigoriy Mymryk. "Your parents are fanatics," he told us with disgust. "They are ignorant people. We want to educate you." I was a strong student, but Mymryk did not allow me to participate in the various educational competitions and other school activities.

One teacher was a saving grace. Her name was Anna Lukinichna, and I remember her with love and gratitude. Some of her relatives had been subjected to oppression, so she understood our plight and treated us with respect and compassion. She especially liked my calligraphy. Despite the headmaster's prohibitions, she sent my works to regional student competitions. She possessed the heart of a true teacher and left an indelible mark upon my heart to this day.

Reading was my love, despite the obstacles I faced in school, and I adored Russian language and Russian literature. I spent hours reading in the school library and was greatly impressed by the classics—Pushkin, Gogol, Lermontov, Dostoyevsky, Nekrasov, and Turgenev. I was enamored by Dostoyevsky's rich prose and his courageous and freedom-loving heart and mind.

Teachers told me it was good to keep reading. "If you proceed with your studies," they said, "all of your religious prejudices, instigated by your fanatical parents, will soon dissipate." But their predictions did not come true.

※ ※ ※

The year 1951 was a tragic one in my family's history. On Ascension Day, two of my brothers, Vladimir and Paul, died giving their lives trying to save our Uncle Ivan, my father's brother-in-law.

Every religious holiday, our Uncle Ivan smoked pork shoulders and other cuts of meat for family and friends after church. The smoker was primitive, an underground cellar about ten feet deep. That morning Uncle Ivan went to check on the meats that had been slowly smoking throughout the night

After he went in, he realized that gas had accumulated during the night and had become poisonous. He screamed and fell on the ground, unconscious. His wife heard the screams and called for help, at which point Vladimir, who was recently married and whose wife was expecting, ran to the cellar and jumped in. In just a few minutes he too was unconscious. Paul, eighteen, jumped in to save them both.

Many of my family members had run to help. Paul put a rope around their bodies and other family members up above were trying to pull them up to safety. He knew he had little time, mere minutes, before he himself would be overcome. Yet tragically, the rope wasn't strong enough and didn't withstand the pressure, breaking apart. "Why have you given me a rotten rope?" Paul shouted. "Time is running out!" By the time someone brought another rope, Paul, Vladimir, and Uncle Ivan were all dead.

On their gravestones were these words from Scripture: "Greater love has no one than this, that one lay down his life for his friends" (John 15:13).

A Miraculous Story of Uncle Andrew

Uncle Andrew, my father's brother, was a foreman in the kolkhoz. He was a strict and extremely critical man with no compassion, even for his relatives. He was very hard on us children when he saw our cows wandering in the grain fields or sugar beet plantations. Aunt Yelena, his wife, was rude and harsh. She drank heavily, surpassing the village men when it came to drinking at parties. They both openly despised our family, particularly Father.

For quite a while, Aunt Yelena had harbored a plan to harm our church. One evening, she came to a service that was held in the house of new believers. There sat humble people, her neighbors and relatives, singing hymns. The Holy Spirit had other plans, grabbing hold of Aunt Yelena's heart through the music. She fell to her knees, wept loudly, and confessed that she had come to cause harm to the believers, but God had stopped her.

After her reconciliation with God, she began to share her faith at home and in the village telling everybody of God's love and mercy. Of course, Uncle Andrew was livid. "Do you understand what you have done?" he screamed. "You have disgraced me before the entire village. I shall not tolerate such shame. Or else you know what I will do, don't you?"

Aunt Yelena was calm. "Andy, do I really stand before you worse than I was before? Now, we shall live real lives. My love for you and for our sons will grow even greater!" But he forbade her to attend church services. Just as stubbornly, Aunt Yelena and the church prayed and fasted for Uncle Andrew.

When she told him she was going to be baptized, he forbade it. "The day you get baptized, I shall kill both you and your priest, Daniel. It is he who has driven you mad! I warned him many times: Don't play with fire!" (Since Russia, or Ukraine, was predominantly

Russian Orthodox, nonbelievers referred to all clergy as "priests." Oftentimes, calling someone a "priest" was a sarcastic or humiliating remark.)

Aunt Yelena prepared herself to be baptized. Infuriated, Uncle Andrew poured kerosene around the house the believers used as a church building. He intended to burn the house with the believers inside, including his wife, but two villagers caught him in time. My father, worried about Aunt Yelena, suggested she wait a year to be baptized to give her husband a chance to calm down.

But Aunt Yelena was clear: "I am not going to delay, I have made my decision before God. Whether death or life waits for me, I want to accomplish God's will."

On the following Sunday morning, Yelena and some believers went by train to a nearby village where she was to be baptized. The village was twenty-five miles away from Kapitanovka. She returned home at about one o'clock in the morning, approaching her house with anxiety and fear. The door was slightly opened when she entered. In the moonlight flooding the room, she saw a gun on the table.

"Andy?"

Silence followed, and she entered the bedroom where Uncle Andrew was sleeping. She lay down beside him, terrified but exhausted. She had begun to doze when suddenly she heard her husband shouting. "Yelena, get up! God does exist! He really is alive! Come, let's pray!"

Frightened, Aunt Yelena jumped out of bed. "What has happened to you, Andrew? What's wrong with you?"

He told her that he had planned to pretend to sleep, thinking about how to kill her and her fellow believers. But before she came home, the room had suddenly filled with light and he saw Jesus standing before him. "Andrew, why are you persecuting me?" Uncle Andrew's heart was pierced.

Soon afterward, they came to visit us in our village, six miles away. Father was working near the house when he saw Andrew and Yelena approaching. Father was bewildered. What could possibly bring Andrew to his home? As he got closer, Uncle Andrew shouted through tears. "Daniel, please forgive me. God is alive! He does exist. I have seen Him today. He appeared to me. Please, forgive me!"

They entered the house. Mom was already fidgeting near the stove. All of us began to pray, weeping and praising God for the miracle that He performed for Uncle Andrew. Afterward, he became an earnest worker for the church and was elected to be a minister.

3

A Young Man's Choice

IN 1953, JOSEPH STALIN DIED. He had been a monster, a mass murderer, and the initiator of all the horrific persecution Christians in Russia faced for twenty-four years. Since 1929, he ordered churches closed, destroyed, or burned down. Many of the Orthodox priests and Evangelical Christian believers were arrested and exiled to Siberia. Those believers who remained had to worship God secretly.

I was seventeen when Stalin died. Our teacher told us "the great leader" and "the father of all times and all nations" had died. She fell on the floor, sobbing uncontrollably. Meanwhile, my fellow students were devastated. "What will we do? What is going to happen to us? We have lost our father! The sun rises from behind the walls of the Kremlin!" And on and on they went, crushed by a tyrant's death. Mournful music was played continually.

During his time in power, everything in Russia was about honoring "Comrade Stalin." It was a cult, a new religion.

In my family, we were happy this evil man, who murdered millions, was dead. God had struck down the despot, at long last. "How the oppressor has ceased, and how fury has ceased! . . . Sheol from beneath is excited over you to meet you when you come" (Isa. 14:4, 9).

We did not show our feelings in the classroom, but when we returned home, the entire family fell to our knees and gave thanks to Almighty God. We believed that a new day would come; and our brothers and sisters in Christ would return home from prisons to see freedom again.

It's impossible to overestimate the terror this man wrought. Literally, people were condemned to death for picking frozen potatoes from winter fields, or searching for little ears of wheat that fell on the road from trucks. They were grabbed from their beds late at night and taken captive because envious acquaintances lied about them. Folks working on the collective farms were forced to pay backbreaking taxes on everything they possessed, trapped there forever because they were never given identification papers.

Millions were tortured or imprisoned and fear ruled. In each family, there was someone who was imprisoned or had been imprisoned. A popular tattoo on the shoulders of those who had been imprisoned read, "The one who wasn't [in prison], will soon be; the one who was, will never forget."

The nation's most talented people—the most educated, artistic, and gifted—were Stalin's pet targets. A popular prison song went like this: "Taganka [a prison in Moscow], I am your permanent prisoner. My youth and my talents perish within your walls!"

Famine, tyranny, gross injustice—these were the hallmarks Russia was known for!

After Stalin's death, amnesty was proclaimed for a time. Many of the prisoners were set free, joyfully returning home to their families who had long been waiting for their release. Yes, for a time, we had a taste of freedom.

An Even Greater Freedom

In the spring of 1953, after the tyrant's death and cruel winter chills, nature came alive with bird's singing and sunlight peeking through the trees. It all felt like God was smiling on me. Nature's glory reminded me of Christ's greatness and power, and I desired for my life to be like a garden of sweet-smelling trees for Him. One afternoon, as I sat under a blossoming pear tree, I knew it was time to give Him my heart and life.

I knelt down on the ground and began to confess my sinfulness and my need for a Savior. Words of repentance poured from my heart, and I am not ashamed to say tears also poured down my face. God revealed himself to me on that day. I now understood that the death of Christ had paid for my sins, once and forever.

"Precious Jesus, you are my Savior, and I am your son forever. Forgive me and wash me with your blood. I will always follow you, wherever my path may lead. I devote my whole life and promise to be faithful for the rest of my days."

From my childhood, I read the Bible and knew much about God. But that day, God revealed the truth to me through the Holy Spirit. For the first time in my life I knew that God was near me. My heart was filled with triumph. The light of God's truth illuminated the darkest corners of my heart. An indescribable joy filled my soul when I realized that now I was God's very own child.

University Enrollment

Since my childhood, I dreamed of the sea. As a young schoolboy, I read many books and stories about explorers and world travelers, far-away lands and oceans. With fascination I read *The Children of Captain Grant* by Jules Verne that took me to distant places around the world, and my love for the sea grew more and more. Finally, I stood in front of the university on 34 Mechnikov Street, in beautiful Odessa, in a park with a fountain encircled by roses and jasmine. For a country boy, it was wonderful to find a piece of nature in the heart of the city.

That day in 1955, I submitted my papers to enter the Engineer University of the Navy (or Naval Academy). That I was allowed to apply was a miracle, for I was not a member of the Komsomol

(Communist Union of Youth). Eighteen applicants vied for one spot in the Academy, and the odds were against me snagging it. Yet God guided me and allowed me to win the place at the university—how grateful and excited I was!

The first day of the school year arrived and I sat in the auditorium, dressed in my student's uniform and listened to my very first lecture. Everything was exhilarating to me—the auditoriums, laboratories, and testing pools for miniature models of ships.

As first-year students, we were recruited to work in the kolkhoz; this was referred to as our "break." Our group went to the village of Roksolany in the Artsizsky region, where we harvested corn and grapes. The job was not new to me. But for the young men from the city, it was much harder. But, step by step, they got used to the work.

We all eagerly waited for our first practical training course when we would be out on the open waters, sailing under the starry skies on the silvery, foamy waves of the Black Sea. The SS *Admiral Nakhimov*, a seven-deck vessel and the flagship of the Black Sea steamship line, was our ship. Our first route was a six-day round trip from Odessa to Batumi, a main port city on the southwest coast of the Black Sea north of Turkey.

My soul always sang out on the sea, and I felt freer than I'd ever felt. Climbing high to the boat deck, I found it to be empty and peaceful. There I could get on my knees and talk to God.

It is impossible to describe the beauty of the early morning and rising of the sun, casting its bright rays from behind mountains, by the shores of Yalta. Dolphins accompanied our ship, playfully jumping and diving in the water.

We began our training as sailors, then boatswains, then guards, and eventually as captains steering the ship (my favorite part). My favorite room on the ship was the musical room, decorated with Persian carpets, paintings by famous artists, luxurious furniture, and a beautiful grand piano and other musical instruments.

Once, the president of the Democratic Republic of Vietnam, Ho Chi Minh, was our passenger. As I was standing on duty by the steering wheel, he approached me, asking questions in broken Russian about my life as a student. I noticed the KGB officers watching us, but at the time thought nothing of it. A year later, they reminded me of that five-minute conversation with the Vietnamese leader.

In the Open Sea

As a captain's assistant, I was given the privilege of inviting up to five of my friends on board to sail with us. I often invited young believers like myself, and we had opportunities to share the way of salvation and God's love with the other passengers.

In the port of Batumi, young believers there would arrange meetings with unbelievers, and we spent entire nights talking. In the morning, I would continue my work, taking passengers aboard and sailing back from Batumi north along the seacoast to Sukhumi, then to Sochi, Yalta, and finally back to Odessa.

One morning I was late for departure. The moorings had been taken up and the ship's ladder removed. My new friends had accompanied me to the pier. The captain took pity on me and commanded the ship to go back. When I scrambled up the ladder onto the ship, he was a bit confused.

"It's your first trip here and you have so many new friends already?"

This would become something everyone on the ship would notice, how I would make friends in every seaport. It became a wonderful way to share with them about Christianity.

I was sad to see my days on the ship come to an end. Practical training finished, and I returned to my everyday life, attending lectures, conducting laboratory studies, and participating in scientific conferences.

The First Mission

During the time I attended school, I spent all my free time in youth ministry. In those days, young people treated their elders and those in church leadership with honor and respect. There was unity and mutual trust between the younger and older generations, something I think is essential for a healthy church.

But it wasn't easy for anyone, young or old, to serve God openly. In those days, there was a definite choice to be made, to either be silent and escape any persecution or to be bold and suffer for Christ's sake.

Many young people were very worried about what would happen if they didn't cooperate with the government, agreeing not to worship Christ. But these extraordinary young people decided to defend the purity of God's teaching, bravely committing themselves to press on despite many barriers. As a leader in the church, I rejoiced at the fact that God's true children had purposely decided to live a victorious life.

In 1958, young believers of the Peresyp church and I organized our first mission, despite the fact that atheistic authorities made it clear we would be arrested if caught. It was called The Good Samaritan.

We wanted to spread the gospel in both word and deed, helping people in any way we found, hoping our works would say more than our words. We did even the smallest things with great love and enthusiasm. A passage from an article in the magazine *A Young Communist* illustrates this (we are referred to as "sectarians"):

> A certain girl cut off her hand with a circular saw. After a few hours some sectarians came to the hospital. Her people took two days to come visit, and then only came twice. But the sectarians stayed by her side, bringing her butter, fruits, flowers, proclaiming, "No, no! You shouldn't thank us, for we are your brothers and sisters! It is our duty!" They would talk about their gospel later, whenever they had the chance. After working long days, the sectarian girls would visit the sick ones and assist helpless old women, bringing them water, washing their laundry, cooking dinner and even preparing firewood for the coming winter.

One day we came to a village to help an old couple dig in their vegetable garden. We hadn't even completed half the job when militia arrived, and we were taken to the militia department with dirt on our hands.

"Is it illegal to help old, helpless citizens? Does Soviet legislation prohibit it?" we asked.

"The state does it, and if you break the law once more, you will go on trial."

But their threats did not stop us in doing good for others.

Just One Night

I joyfully continued my studies, relishing the chance to learn all about ships, shipbuilding, and the nautical life. Yet I had a growing sense that soon it would be taken away from me.

My beliefs and growing influence on the other students did not go unnoticed. Surveillance over my activities was becoming more intense with each day. My teachers, who liked me, encouraged me to keep my beliefs to myself. "Many people believe in God deep in their souls. We also make the sign of the cross before going to bed or before having meals." They urged me to graduate from the university first and then if I must, share my faith. (Prompted at the time by these developments, I began to search out a suitable trade to pay the bills if I was not allowed to graduate and become an engineer. Soon I became certified to operate a crane.)

The dean of the university began a campaign to make me change my ways. I was lectured, brainwashed, bribed and threatened. There was a cartoon in the student newspaper, depicting me standing on my knees and stretching my hands to the sky. It read, "Aspiring to heavenly heights."

The KGB officers were, of course, the most eager to "reeducate" me. I particularly remember Kolutchiy, whose last name meant "prickly." Caustic and surly, he lived up to his name as he made my life as uncomfortable as possible.

Finally, I was given an ultimatum: choose between God and my desired profession. I would make my choice at a student assembly the next day.

My heart was heavy, and I spent the night in agonizing prayer. "God, what am I supposed to do?" My beautiful dream of becoming a ship's engineer had come true, against the odds, and now it was slipping away.

My Choice

The university's assembly hall was filled with the noise of chattering young men and women. The top school officials were all there, and even the undersecretary of the Soviet Navy was present. The faculty dean, a gentle man named Mironenko, was the first to speak:

"Joseph Bondarenko studies well. He is a member of the Students' Scientific Council and has a few award papers for his scientific work on shipbuilding. The Soviet power gave him a great opportunity. But he doesn't get along with the ideology of the Soviet society. We have learned he believes in God, and has some sort of an important position in a mission, as well as in an unregistered Baptist church. The knowledge he acquires within our educational facility, he uses for accomplishing religious goals, not for the betterment of the Soviet society."

The undersecretary of the Soviet Navy spoke next:

"Our Communist Party and our government do their best for our young people to share the right ideology and to scrupulously observe Lenin's precepts. I would like to have such a good worker as Bondarenko in our Ministry, but when I offered him this opportunity he refused. Some strive for such a position for years, but he refused. I can't understand his refusal. There is a happy future right there in front of him, but he is shutting the door."

The students and the teachers listened closely, understanding my fate rested on this statesman's decision.

I was the last to speak. I rose from my seat and went forward, where I was met by hundreds of pairs of eyes. Their faces wore a mixture of curiosity and hostility, though some looked at me with eyes of compassion. There was a lump in my throat, and I tried to clear it before I began:

"Dear students and teachers, for four years, I have been impatiently waiting for graduation and my shipbuilding engineer's diploma. I like the university, my studies, and my profession very much. I am very grateful to the teachers and the administration here for the possibility to study. But I have been asked to make a choice—graduate from here and become a qualified engineer, or renounce God. My desire is to graduate, but I cannot renounce my God."

The crowd became agitated. The teachers sitting in the presidium were whispering to each other, and some students shouted, "What is wrong with his faith? Let him study. He is a good student and a supportive mate!"

When everybody was quiet, I went on speaking:

"I want everybody to realize that serving God and my neighbors is the very goal of my life. I can't repudiate the One who gave His life for me. I can't give up my beliefs for the sake of a diploma."

"Bondarenko, take your seat. It is not a house of prayer here," the dean interrupted me. "Comrades! Joseph Bondarenko will not be allowed to defend his diploma project. He is hereby excluded from the university for spreading an ideology which is harmful for the Soviet society."

To be honest, I felt pity for him and the others who had condemned me. My generation had been disfigured by Communism, a religion designed to control people like mindless animals.

Later, as we were leaving the assembly hall, several of my fellow students took me aside to encourage me. "Well done, Joseph," they whispered. "Take courage for what is to come."

4

The First Arrest

AFTER BEING KICKED OUT OF UNIVERSITY, I began to work as a portal crane operator in a seaport. Despite my disappointment over my forced dismissal, I liked my job. My "booth" rose forty feet above the ground and seemed to bring me closer to the heavens.

From that height, the boundless sea and endless transparent skies provided a view I never became tired of. Inside, there was a blessed, deep silence, unscathed by the longshoremen's foul language below. It was cozy and warm, with plenty of time for meditation and prayer. During my lunch break I could read and nap.

In summer, when other crane operators enjoyed their vacations, I used to cover their shifts on floating cranes weighing hundreds of tons. This job entailed lots of responsibility, but the salary was bigger. God did not leave me, and he met all my earthly needs.

But the KGB wasn't content to let me do my job peacefully. They worried that I might tell foreigners arriving at the port to board ships about how badly believers were treated. I was fired, but managed to find a job soon thereafter as a crane operator on a construction site. Even so, I knew the KGB was watching me constantly.

The Baptism

Even baptism, a simple act of obedience to Christ, was extremely dangerous and had to be done in the dark of night. At that time, pastors and lay leaders were arrested and placed in prisons and hard labor camps if they were caught. Publication of Christian magazines and books ceased, as did seminary and Bible courses of all kinds. In the mid-1930s, almost all of the five thousand Evangelical churches had closed. By 1956–59, the authorities ramped up their efforts to enslave and crush the church. God's people were placed in a furnace of sufferings.

So it was no small undertaking when I decided to obey God in baptism. It was a moonlit night on June 5, 1960, the night some of my friends and I were baptized secretly in a lake near my home village. The moonlight shone on every surface and seemed to reflect God's pleasure in our decision. At about 2 a.m., we reached the shores of the beautiful lake, having crept and even crawled along the path, in fear the militia would hear us. As each one of us was immersed into the water, we answered the minister's questions: "Yes, I believe. I promise to serve you forever, oh Lord!"

On the shore we were greeted with joy by our friends and family. Despite the tension and anxiety of being caught, I felt unusually lighthearted and joyful. It was an unforgettable moment of pure devotion to the God we loved. We stole back to one of our homes; the windows, as in war times, were covered tightly with dark paper and blankets. There, in the presence of our families and some of the friends who had come, we participated in the first Lord's Supper of our lives. This divine memory would comfort and sustain me in the hard times ahead.

Before the Arrest

By the end of 1961, there were more and more reports about my activities, both to the public prosecutor's office and to the KGB. Magazines and newspapers, such as *Atheist Agitator's Notebook*, mentioned me by name and called me and my friends "religious fanatics," who "openly don't acknowledge the Soviet legislation of religious cults." We were accused of using Bible study groups to lure new members into our group, and of "studying the Bible and Christian literature."

The government spread vicious propaganda about Christians, Baptists in particular, through various radio and television programs and in the print media. They pointed the finger at us as being barbarians and fanatics, going so far as to accuse us of child sacrifice as a regular church practice. Many believed the lies that were spread, and contempt and hatred for Christians grew.

As one of the leaders in the Underground Baptist Church, I was a special target of the KGB, which saved their harshest oppression for pastors, church leaders, and those Christians who would not keep silent about their beliefs.

For example, if a lay Christian was in fact arrested in those days, the detention was usually for fifteen days, and then they were released. The Soviets used this as a scare tactic to keep them in line. Other common methods they used to control believers included the threat of being fired, taking away privileges such as access to vacation spots, or denying them bonuses at work, or actually having people fired from their jobs. One of the biggest measures used was deny an active believer access to higher education.

Criminal accusations and intense prison time were reserved for "highly dangerous individuals posing a threat to Soviet ideology," such as myself and other Christian leaders who were active at this time.

Yes, I was considered "highly dangerous." In 1960s, before my arrest (and then again years later after my second prison term), I was on the KBG's Ten Most Wanted criminals list. For one reason, I was the national youth leader of the Underground Baptist Church and taught young people and children the Bible. Since these youth were the future generation of the Communist society, Soviet government didn't tolerate anyone teaching anything to younger people but their ideological ideas. In those days, teaching the Bible to young people, minors, and children was a serious and punishable crime.

The Baptist church was divided into registered and unregistered segments. Those churches registered by the government were less persecuted, whereas unregistered churches were persecuted because of their brave resistance to the atheistic Soviet intrusion into the spiritual matters of the church.

Several months later, I became a national figure for the Church Council of the Evangelical Baptist Church, known as the Underground Baptist movement. I was among the first of several people who started the "Initiative Group," an underground movement that encouraged all believers to stand up for their faith and against the Soviet government's control and intervention within the church. This movement changed the history of the Evangelical Church in the Soviet Union and was the cause of much-needed publicity in the West. It stirred the hearts of Soviet expatriates abroad and gave them hope of changing the direction in the country. The expats saw the real power of Christians to stand up for freedom, which was the forward motion needed for them to start campaigning in absentia for religious freedoms and human rights in the Soviet Union. Not many are aware of this vital role of believers in the overall battle for freedoms in the Soviet Union.

But the main reason I was on the most-wanted list was because I had been among the organizers of a delegation of five hundred believers in Small Square in Moscow to protest against injustice done towards believers and people of free will, including unjust imprisonment of thousands of believers of all faiths and inhumane treatment of them in prisons throughout Russia and Soviet republics.

My First Sight of the KGB Office

In January 1962, I was called for the first time to the KGB office. After being interrogated, two officers began to beat me, punching and kicking me. "Why are you beating me?" I was confused and terrified, as I protected my face as best I could with my hands. The two officers seemed to be enjoying themselves. "Don't you know? You are a Baptist believer, and a very stubborn one. People like you should be killed!" Every word that came out of their mouths was a curse or an angry accusation. "Why are you not turning your other cheek to us? Isn't it written in your Bible?"

As the blows landed, one after the other, I was in a haze of pain and fear. There's no way I would be let go after this, I thought. But astonishingly, after beating me to a pulp, they let me go late that night. Utterly humiliated and broken in body and spirit, I stumbled home and dropped into my bed.

Somehow I knew the next time the KGB came for me, I would not get off so easily. A month later, subpoena in hand, I arrived at the prosecutor's office in Odessa, where I was interrogated, beaten, and thrown into prison for the first time.

The Prison in Odessa

The prison I was brought to was built in the eighteenth century, in the times of the Russian tsarina Catherine the Great. The reception building was actually beautiful on the outside, with a high dome-shaped roof. Inside, the floors were divided by a kind of metal mesh to prevent prisoners from escaping or embracing death by suicide. It was both scary and horrible, like something out of a nightmare.

We passed through three iron doors into a narrow corridor dimly lit by a single crimson light. Doors, doors, and more doors— they were all bolted with huge locks. I heard rumbling from inside, like the humming of bees in their beehive.

Finally, yet another door opened to cell #5, and I entered this cold, damp, and gloomy little room. It was a quarantine cell. Apparently, it was dinner time, and a disgusting smell of rotten fish began to filter into the cell. A feeding trough opened. "Enjoy your *balanda*!" a disembodied voice said. (*Balanda* was a tasteless porridge made of a variety of low quality grains.)

I couldn't touch the "dinner." The smells of the rotting fish, the dampness, and the *parasha* (a big bucket used as a toilet in Soviet prisons) made eating seem impossible. I was unable to eat the prison "meals" for the first three or four days, but after a while I forced myself to eat because I didn't want to starve to death.

At bedtime, I heard the terrible clanging of iron beds all over the prison. My bed was nothing but a board of iron strips welded together. Lying down on it was extremely uncomfortable as the sharp edges dug into my flesh.

I spent seven intolerable days in solitary confinement, getting up at 6 a.m. and not being able to lie down until 10 p.m. Only standing and sitting on the floor were permitted. To use the bathroom, I had to move silently through the corridor with my hands behind my back, escorted by the armed guard.

After seven days I was taken to the common cell on the second floor. The windows were covered in iron bars and a huge wooden board designed to obscure all but a tiny piece of sky. Irons beds were affixed to the wall with hooks, and could be let down only between 10 p.m. and 6 a.m.

On my fourth day in the prison I was called to the interrogator, who said they had reliable information "concerning my criminal activity." The interrogator, piecing together random bits of information, had concluded that my fellow believers and I were planning a "congress," or a conference, to elect new ministers who would operate without any approval from local authorities.

"We shall arrange a congress for you believers alright—in prison." His voice was low and threatening. "Hiding the truth is useless. We are aware of your plans to work among the young people and brainwash them into buying your beliefs, all for the benefit of American imperialists."

I tried to share my faith with him, and he was oddly receptive. "You know, I appreciate your openness and conviction," he said quietly. "Yet I believe the consequences will be very serious for you. Who will help you?"

"Only God," I said calmly.

He had had enough. When my escort took me back to my cell, the interrogator shouted at me down the corridor. "We shall see how your God will help you!"

Interrogations of all kinds followed, and I was asked repeatedly to denounce my faith—or else. Yet my lot was not as bad as that experienced by believers during Stalin's reign of terror. Those believers were interrogated day and night (mine were during the day only), with KGB officers working in shifts around the clock. The prisoners went without food or sleep, only to be returned to their cells and made to stand up straight without moving for hours. If they fainted or stumbled, they were beaten. Knowing of the courageous example of these believers strengthened me, and I prayed for the will to hold on.

❊ ❊ ❊

My friend Nikolai Pavlovitch was also in the same prison at the same time; he was accused of the same crimes as me. We were undoubtedly worried; prison camp was waiting for us, and we were to leave our families, our church, and our friends. But when he and I would get the rare chance to talk, we resolved that we would fight the good fight together, Nikolai and I and our fellow believers outside the prison walls. We mused that though the atheists thought the church would be scattered by persecution, the opposite had happened, and the church had grown even stronger.

Soon after we were taken prisoner, word began to spread about our resolve in the face of dire opposition. One day, we received a secret message from a group of thieves highly respected in the world of criminals. They were referred to as "The Real Men." "We appreciate the courage you have shown speaking against the militiamen and the Soviet 'host,'" the note read. "Don't give up!"

Of course, word got out to prison officials that Nikolai and I were speaking to others inside about God. They were not pleased, to say the least, and this caused our fellow convicts to respect us and listen to our message all the more. The prisoners had many questions for us:

"Why are you here?"

"Where is your God?"

"Why does He let such a terrible thing happen to you, His servants?"

We invited such questions and tried our best to answer them.

"God wants to bring you his message of grace through us," we replied. "You might never have heard of God's forgiveness and love if you hadn't met us inside."

Our discussions often lasted up to bedtime. Nikolai and I would lie on our plank beds, praying that God would get through to them.

Sadly, it wasn't long before Nikolai and I were separated in different cells. As the KGB continued to investigate us, I learned that they considered me a *parovoz*, or a "locomotive," the first one to be accused on a case. Nikolai was next in line, and we were both accused of "involving minors in criminal activity, such as church services." This was considered a terrible crime.

Days in the Cell

They moved me and the other prisoners around quite a bit. The first thing any believer did upon entering a new cell was pray; this made meeting and communicating with our cellmates easier. On one occasion, I was moved to a cell with twelve others, and as usual, I was asked where I was from and what I had been accused of.

When I told them of my crime, one cellmate asked me, "If you are God's man, why have they imprisoned you with us? They don't lock up "holy people!"

Another cellmate asked if it was true that I offered children as sacrifices. This was just one of many heinous accusations being perpetuated by atheist authorities and media.

One prisoner, though, voiced a different view: "These believers are political prisoners courageously opposing the Soviet power and their laws prohibiting religious activity." Many of the inmates actually admired us for bucking the Soviet powers. One time a *pakhan*, a kind of crime lord or "godfather," feared and respected by all, ordered the other inmates to give me the bed closer to the window, moving others closer to the *parasha*, which was emitting revolting odors night and day.

The nights were the worst. Those who had been condemned to die by firing squad knew that on any given night, it could be their turn to be taken out of the cell and shot to death. The screams we heard as these prisoners were on their way to execution raised the hairs on our necks. "I want to live!" was one we frequently heard, but the most shocking of all was "Mama!" As the poet Nikolai Nekrasov wrote, "We love our sister, our wife, our father, but in torment we remember our mother."

5

A Verdict

THE DAYS PASSED WITH ACHING slowness. There was one window in the cell, and through finger-thick bars and wooden slats I could see a tiny piece of a blue sky. I stared at that beautiful patch of blue all the time, thinking about my loved ones and friends who were free under that same sky somewhere. The heavens were above us all, and even though the authorities had locked us up behind thick concrete walls and iron bars, they could not prevent us from seeing that slice of heaven.

On the other side of the cell, there was a big heavy door made of iron sheets, fitted with a small peephole so the guards walking by could check up on us. Below it sat a feeding trough hanging on hinges. When it was opened, it looked like a small serving table on which they "served" rotten fish and other food. We called it the "devil's mouth."

Even inside these iron walls there were ways to get messages to others on the inside. "To send a horse" meant to send a note. Fastening a thread from a sock to the note, you used twigs or spoons to push the note through the iron bars, lowering it or lifting it to the floor below or above. A knock on the pipes or the ceiling gave the signal that there was a message, or a "horse" waiting. Many notes were passed to all floors of the prison in this manner. This was how I discovered that Nikolai Shevchenko, a pastor in our community and a spiritual father to me, was also in the prison.

Through a note, we agreed that when he was going along the corridor to wash or go to the toilet, he would knock the floor three times with his walking stick, which would be his special greeting to me. How those knocks encouraged me, and how I listened for them among the screams and curses of the prison!

Three knocks bolstered my spirits as I thought about the earlier days of freedom when we worked together in ministry, and this reminded me that there were many people on the outside praying for us both. God had not forgotten me, and he had heard my cries for help. I remembered David's words in Psalm 94:19: "When my anxious thoughts multiply within me, Your consolations delight my soul."

The First Day of Trial

The investigation was over. I had been charged with antisocial activity, religious agitation of young people, holding home church services, and helping the poor.

After a ten-day period in which I was allowed to look over the charges, a court date was set for August 9, 1962. Nikolai and I were herded into a *voronok*, in which we were driven to the court. On the way there, we were forbidden to speak or to sit down.

The trial took place at a worker's club in a factory on Moskovskaya Street in Odessa. Many supporters were gathered there, including friends and believers from various churches. Some of my family came, including my father, Sasha, Vasily, and his wife, Tamara. Sasha was pregnant, and when she entered the building a militia man kicked her belly with his foot. Fortunately, she did not lose her baby.

About ten thousand people worked at the factory, among them many atheists who slandered believers. Because they had spread the rumor that Nikolai and I had sacrificed children, there was also a large crowd of people who were very hostile towards us. When we arrived in the *voronok*, this crowd blocked our way into the courtyard of the building.

People rocked the vehicle, shouting angrily. "Child killers! They should be put to death without trial!" Militia men waved their guns at them, demanding we be let through, to no avail. Finally, the *voronok* was backed out of there and driven to a nearby militia office, where our guard duty was doubled. Still, the enraged mob would not allow us to get through.

Unsettled by this horde, the militia put us both in wrist manacles, which were excruciatingly tight and caused unbearable pain at the slightest movement. Finally, someone came up with the idea to lead the procession with an asphalt-paving machine, to confuse the throng.

When they realized they had been duped, the crush of people grew even more furious, screaming and throwing themselves at the barred gates. At the same time, our supporters sang hymns and threw flowers under the *voronok*.

Inside the courtroom, the rows of seats were filled with militia men, soldiers, and representatives of the Communist Party, Komsomol activists, and voluntary patrol members. Not a single believer was let in.

The names of the judge, two jurymen, a public prosecutor, a secretary, and a public accuser were read out loud, followed by our charges and the names of the eighty-four witnesses.

The proceedings were being filmed, and hot and unbearably bright lights were focused on us.

The judge asked if we had any requests, and we said yes. "Why aren't our friends and relatives let into the hall? This trial should be broadcast outside the courtroom, so those gathered outside can hear what's going on inside."

The judge replied that more people couldn't be let into the hall because it would be a fire safety violation. To protest, we refused to answer any of the judge's questions for about fifteen minutes, at which point we repeated our request to let our supporters inside.

Eventually, after a couple of episodes of us refusing to speak, the judge agreed that my brother Vasily could make up a list of fifty people who would be let inside. Astonishingly, the judge also granted our second request and agreed to broadcast the proceedings.

We were appointed an attorney to represent us, even though we knew they wouldn't truly represent us.

The judge read the indictment, which accused us of antisocial activity, preaching, organizing Bible studies, and diverting young people from "public activities."

During the break, we met our attorney. She had studied the case and she didn't see that there were real grounds for us being arrested. "It's a shame that young people like you are being imprisoned without committing any crime," she said, to our great surprise. This lawyer promised to do what she could do decrease our sentences.

After the break, it was announced that our spiritual activity and ministering to the poor were recognized as a crime, as described in article 209, part I, of the Criminal Code of the Ukrainian Soviet Socialist Republic. Our ministry efforts supposedly made us guilty of leading an antisocial, parasitic way of life, thus posing a threat to Soviet society.

People standing outside and listening to the trial, however, were beginning to see that the facts didn't add up. It quickly became obvious that we hadn't sacrificed children or committed any other heinous crime. "Is it a crime to hold prayer services?" someone was heard to say. It was obvious to almost everyone that the trial had been fabricated for the purposes of Soviet publicity.

A group of students in the hall began to protest loudly. "These men are accused of believing in God! What a farce!"

The public accuser lost his patience. "Don't you understand? They are American spies and traitors spreading false ideology to our young people, our future!"

When the authorities realized that broadcasting the trial was actually changing the minds of those who had been against us, they stopped broadcasting and filming immediately. This trial was not going according to the KGB's prescribed plot—not one little bit.

At the end of the first day, we were led back to the *voronok*. This time, we were let through with no problem. Our friends and family and other Christians again sang hymns and threw flowers under the truck as we were being driven out of the courtyard. Later we found out that several of them had been arrested and thrown in jail for up to fifteen days.

The Second Day

The next morning we were given our day's food ration: a herring and a 10-ounce piece of bread. To our surprise and joy, the court was transporting us in a militia bus, which was much more comfortable than the airless *voronok*. Once again, Nikolai and I couldn't talk, but we were happy to see each other and the streets we used to walk down many times. As we passed the old seaport where I had my student's training, I said good-bye in my mind. I wondered if this would be the day our freedom would be stolen forever.

The "witnesses" that day were again unable to give any convincing testimony. Most of them had never seen us or heard our preaching and "speeches defaming the power of the Soviets." Of course, they weren't real witnesses but carefully chosen and instructed atheists. Fifty out of the eighty-four witnesses were rather quickly brought before the court, as they had nothing useful to say.

Some believers were called to testify, and their accounts were brief and honest, holding nothing back and quoting Scripture when they could.

That evening when we were taken back to the prison, rumors about the trial were buzzing all over the building. Somehow everybody knew about the proceedings and how our fellow believers had welcomed us with flowers and hymns. Any lingering doubts about the horrible things we had been accused of—such as child sacrifice—were banished completely. "If they truly had offered their children as sacrifices, they would have been executed or been thrown in prison for at least fifteen years," the inmates reasoned as they discussed our case.

One of the old-time criminals kept muttering over and over that we had been given the shaft: "It would be clear to a *hedgehog* now that Joseph and Nikolai's case is completely trumped up!"

The Third Day

On the third day of trial, there were so many people—believers and nonbelievers—trying to get inside to watch, the militia were working overtime to keep crowd control. Metallic sheets were hastily welded onto the fence bars, so nobody could see us being taken into the building through the yard.

The witnesses' testimonies continued. The believers were again confident and on track, while the atheists persistently became muddled and aimless as they spit out their lies.

The public accuser obviously wanted blood: his recommendation to the court was to press charges to the full extent of the law—ten years in prison for each of us.

Our defense attorney followed up with her remarks. We were innocent, she said, a fact backed by the weak evidence and insubstantial testimonies against us by the witnesses. We did not deserve to be imprisoned, let alone for ten years.

Finally, I was put on the stand. "Comrade judge! Comrades jurymen! We are accused of involvement and perpetuation of a religious cult. We cannot accept that we have broken any law whatsoever, except that we have served the Lord and taught our children to serve him. How can we suppress our conscience before our children?"

I used my country's own laws to defend myself. "In 1962, a law was ratified in the USSR which read: 'Parents and legal tutors enjoy the right to educate their children in the spirit of their beliefs, and can teach and be taught religion privately.'

"We in no way violated human rights, but you violated the believing parents' rights. We committed no crime and broke no law. The only fault of ours is we were born in a country where there is no freedom of conscience and faith. Any lawyer in any language would say that when laws like these exist and authorities do not observe them, it is called tyranny. It is a disgrace to the Communist regime. The real reason you persecute us is our faith in the living God."

I went on, telling of how I had been persecuted since I was a young boy, and how God had been with me, giving me strength in every trial I faced. "My very life is in His hands. Yes, going to prison for years frightens me, but God will not leave me, and those who want to harm us will bring shame upon themselves."

As I was speaking, the judge repeatedly jumped in, interrupting me impatiently. "This is not the place to preach!" he scolded me. "Keep it to essential issues."

But I had essential things to say, and I kept going despite his frequent reprimands. I used my time on the stand to publicly forgive those who had hurt me physically and otherwise. I also confessed to having done some of the "crimes" of which I was accused, such as leading Bible studies for youth and inviting children to church.

"Let them lie about us in the newspapers," I said. "Our way has been paved by Jesus Christ, who said, 'If they persecuted Me, they will also persecute you.'"

"Bondarenko!" The judge was out of patience. "This is not a house of prayer!" I had my say, so I finished, and Nikolai took the stand.

"I thank God for the privilege given to me, to be judged, not as a thief or bandit, but a Christian believer, His witness," he said calmly. "I believe freedom will come for this country, but if this doesn't happen, I will be quoting Habakkuk the prophet and exulting in the Lord anyway. I am not blaming anybody, nor do I have any doubts concerning my chosen path. I know I am right, so I can look you in the eye with no shame."

After a short break (the court had already decided our sentence before we were called to the stand), the judge read the verdict and our sentence:

"Having considered the facts, according to the Penal Code of the Ukrainian Soviet Socialist Republic, the court has sentenced Bondarenko, Joseph, and Shevchenko, Nikolai, to be deprived of freedom and imprisoned. Bondarenko, Joseph, has been sentenced to five years of imprisonment and three years of exile." Nikolai received four years in prison and four years of exile. The atheists sitting in the hall cheered loudly at the verdict.

The trial had ended, and with it all the strain and uncertainty. Often, knowing the truth is better than wondering about what may happen. Strangely, Nikolai and I both felt at peace, despite the fact that we had received no justice that day. But then again, we never for a minute expected it.

6

An Introduction to Prison Life

LATE THAT SAME NIGHT, we were brought back to Odessa Central Prison. I was given a dirty, bloodstained mattress filled with sawdust, a pillow, a pillowcase, and a sheet. The linens were filthy and smelled rank, but to me it was an upgrade from the prickly plank beds.

However, swarms of bed bugs lived in the bedding, and my nights became hellish episodes of scratching the endless itchy bites all over my body. The sensitive skin around my eyes felt like it was on fire, and I rarely fell asleep before dawn.

The food was horrible, usually a ration of oatmeal we called "horse's joy" and a revolting thick soup of rotten cucumbers and dried potatoes.

Every six months, we were allowed to receive an eleven-pound parcel from loved ones and friends. The rules of what they could send were strict: no fats, only dried brown bread, fish preserves in tomato sauce, stewed vegetables, onion, and garlic. Still, comparatively, we felt like kings when we could eat the contents of those packages.

After a week they began to take me out to work inside a small industrial zone. I was to hammer together wooden boxes for vegetables. The daily quota was large. I had to make sixty boxes a day. It was difficult to fulfill the quota, and for not fulfilling it they reduced my daily ration of porridge and bread even further.

One day, as I was working in the industrial zone, a man who was a "civilian" (a volunteer) came up to me and put two small chocolate bars in my hand. He turned out to be my Christian brother who belonged to the local church of Evangelical Christians; he used to come to the camp twice a month to tune and fix the machine tools. He never told me what his name was, but he used to support me from time to time. I thank God for His faithful servants.

The overseer was a fractious man named Bubitch, who clearly had it in for me from the start. He made his informants watch me closely, and they were highly motivated to get some dirt. If they were to succeed, they could buy some *makhora* (coarse tobacco), and receive an additional ration of bread. I had to be very careful. One of their common tricks used against me and other believers inside was telling us they could deliver messages and notes to people on the outside, which was true, except they didn't mention the fact that every message was copied for the KGB. Many believers' families and Christian friends suffered because of this trick. Once I tried to get a New Testament this way, but it proved impossible. "Anything but the Bible," people would say. I had to make do with verses I knew by heart.

Days off and holidays were particularly lonely and depressing as we weren't taken outside for work or to walk around. The monotony and lack of fresh air would take their toll and some days, sadness squeezed my heart. I would sing hymns in a low, soft voice (such singing was forbidden) and pray like Jabez, that God's hand would be with me and keep me from harm (1 Chron. 4:10). These small practices brought healing and comfort to my heart.

An Extraordinary Vision

I had good days and bad days, and during my darkest times, it felt like God had just disappeared and I was alone. My soul was submerged in darkness. Prison is spiritually black, and it was so hard sometimes to be a light in the midst of constant swearing, filthy jokes and stories, and just foul conduct. Before I fell asleep I would cry out to God for strength to survive.

One night I couldn't fall asleep, when suddenly the dark cell was lit with extraordinary light. I was shocked and frightened by the sight of an old man, an angel, with a shining face, white hair, and a snowy beard. He began counting off some numbers, but the only one that stood out to me was the number three. Confused and scared, I jumped off my bed to ask him what he meant, but he vanished into thin air. "Lord, what does this vision mean?" I whispered, trembling.

I paced my cell excitedly, thinking about the meaning of the vision. Suddenly a thought came to me: "I will leave the prison before the appointed date, in three years instead of eight!" I jumped for joy and then knelt down on the concrete floor to pray. "Lord, it is You who determines my sentence, not the judges. My life is truly in your hands."

Igor

I was moved to another cell, where a young man named Igor was my neighbor. He lashed out immediately the first time he heard me pray. "That was the only thing I have been missing here—your prayers!" he said sarcastically. "I don't want to listen to them. And don't even say the word "God" here! Life is bright and beautiful, and your God has nothing to do with that! The only thing I need is freedom!"

Igor was a secretary of the Komsomol organization at his job, and he had been sentenced ten years for a fight he instigated that had gone wrong. During the fight, his friend had hurt his head and become an invalid.

"Okay," I said quietly. "Then why didn't you use your freedom in a right way?"

This added fuel to his fire.

"The Marxist philosophy is the only right one. Why don't you understand that?" He was livid.

"I think Christian teaching is the most fair and true," I said. "I'm actually here because I defended its principles. *Your* ideology is being forced upon people."

Of course he wasn't buying it.

"The Communist Party is mighty, and we shall build up a bright future for everybody. You are nothing but a fanatic."

It was useless to argue. I decided rather to pray instead.

The next day our argument continued at the washstand, where he swore at me as he dumped the contents of the *parasha* onto me. Though it was humiliating and disgusting, I restrained myself from doing or saying anything.

The conflict became more serious with each passing day. Igor tried to make each day unbearable for me, dumping my soup at dinner, disturbing my sleep by shouting and insulting me. But God gave me the grace to turn the other cheek, and I would share my rations with him, clean the cell, back down to him, and forgive his every attack. I prayed constantly, for him, and for me.

Igor was a nervous man who would anxiously pace across the cell. I guessed that he was worried about having to serve his full ten years, as young people usually did. His situation seemed to be hopeless, and he saw no way out.

"Igor," I said once, "I think your sentence will be reduced to seven years, maybe even five." He ignored me, but I think it gave him a spark of hope. That night he didn't yell at me for praying.

Time went on, and finally he opened up to me. "Tell me, is it true that Christ forgives all the sins?"

"Yes, Igor, and yours, too."

"What a shame I didn't understand that earlier," he said slowly. "I didn't understand anything."

Eventually, the Holy Spirit touched his heart, and Igor could see things clearly. "Forgive me," he said one day, "I treated you badly because the prison officials made me do it. I do not want to live my life messing with other people's minds anymore. I don't want to be at war with God." I could tell this was very difficult for him to say. That night he prayed and asked God's forgiveness, too.

We were friends from then on, even though he felt terribly guilty for the things he had done to me. I forgave him willingly, but he couldn't forgive himself.

Inevitably, the prison authorities caught wind of the changes in Igor. After all, he wasn't fulfilling their orders anymore. One day, we heard a key turning in the lock of the cell's door. My heart gave a start. "Let's go, and bring your things!" I heard a guard bark at me. I grabbed my small knapsack and threw my stuff into it, turning at the door to look at Igor. It was more difficult to part from a fellow believer in prison than it was on the outside.

Igor's eye's filled with tears. "Joseph, thank you," he said. "I met you for a reason, and I will never forget that."

I never saw him again, but I have thought of him many times, wondering about his fate.

7

Four Steps Long and Three Steps Wide

MY INFLUENCE ON IGOR did not go unpunished and I was thrown into solitary confinement. I can still see those dirty grey walls, the iron door with a small window and spy hole, the cement stool and rusty iron bed—nothing but concrete and iron, grey and rust. I used to pace around my cell, measuring it with my steps (four steps long and three steps wide). My feet knew each and every hole in that cement floor.

I often thought about my namesake, Joseph in the Bible, wrongfully accused and thrown in prison, his limbs shackled in iron. Twice a day I was taken to the toilet, which thankfully was quite a distance away. I tried to walk as slowly as possible to make it last.

The highlight of my day by far was my daily walk. As I stretched my legs in the fresh air of the walking yard—more like a parking lot—I was observed by a guard in a watchtower. Not a single blade of grass poked through the cement, and the sky was somewhat obscured by the mesh tarp overhead, but still I craved this change of scenery. Oddly, the rule was to keep your hands behind your back the entire twenty or thirty minutes (I was the only one there!).

One step out of line and they would take away my walking privileges, which was absolutely devastating for me. I lived for those patches of blue sky, the seagulls flying over me, and the beautiful sounds of a steamship's horn. I remembered my days on a steamship in the Black Sea, and each blast of a ship's horn felt like a friend calling out to me.

The most important thing for me to do was not cave in to depression and even madness. I worried that I would forget how to talk, so I quoted Scripture out loud to myself. The worst time of the day was in the evening, after supper, when the silence grew so thick it felt like it could suffocate me. I yearned with all my soul to hear even a single sound other than my own voice.

Yasha

After a time I was moved by *voronok* to a prison camp in Vilkovo, about 128 miles southwest of Odessa, away from the sea and its sounds. But there were compensations at this camp, the first being that I was reunited with Nikolai, although we weren't in the same barrack. I also met Yasha here.

A few hours after getting settled, a tough-looking guy approached me. "Are you a believer?" I said yes, and told him my name. His face was a mixture of joy and fear. "I was told there was a believer on the barge [our transport to the camp, situated on an island]. I heard your friends, the believers, threw flowers at you during your trial," he said, his face still lit by surprise. "Listen, there's something important I need to talk to you about in private."

His name was Jakov Slobodnyuk, "Yasha," and he came from Shevchenko. As he told me his story that night, he could hardly get the words out, because he was so excited. Yasha had grown up in a Christian home but had rejected the faith of his parents. He hung out with a thuggish crowd who respected him because he had scrapped his way to being the most thuggish of them all. His reputation was that of a violent, unruly guy with a fierce temper. You didn't cross Yasha if you wanted to live a long life.

On one occasion, he shot at a brigade leader in the kolkhoz with the intention to kill him. Fortunately, he didn't. For the crime of attempted murder, he received five years in the maximum security prison camp.

Yasha told me of his father, and how he had written him a letter that Yasha had sewed into the padding of his jacket. The letter ended this way: "My son, when your life is hard remember my words and speak to God, who loves you and is waiting for you. Come back to your heavenly Father's house."

Yasha had thought about his father's words countless times, and hardhearted as he had been, now he was ready to respond and return to God. He just needed a guide. "I'm tired of fighting and lying and all the mess," he said. "I want something pure and holy for my life."

There in the boiler room, Yasha knelt down and prayed for forgiveness. "Take me back as your lost son," he prayed softly. "I have done so much harm to You, my parents, and my family. I'm so sorry for it all, and I want to be Yours."

The heavens seemed to open up in that dark boiler room in the middle of the prison camp. We felt God standing between us there, touching us with his nail-scarred hands, blessing us both. I could see clearly in that sacred moment that one reason God had brought me down this hard, rocky path was to help the most broken and hopeless people in society—prisoners. Yasha and I were still locked up, but on the inside we were free.

Baptism in the Prison Camp

Yasha wanted to be baptized almost immediately after believing, but how? It seemed impossible, so we prayed to the God of the possible, who heard us and opened up a way.

It was very risky, but the manager of the washhouse agreed to look the other way while I baptized Yasha in a giant bathtub. Afterward, we had communion together, also a miracle. With great difficulty, we had managed to obtain a small piece of brown bread and a mug of grape juice. How precious were the words of Jesus at the Last Supper: "Do this in remembrance of Me" (Luke 22:19).

"My Lord and my God," Yasha exulted. "My past has been buried forever!"

Yasha and I promised always to pray for one another, and he became one of my closest friends.

Together, we formed the nucleus of a small group of believers at the prison. We were under constant surveillance, but we did our best to meet for prayer and Bible discussions. During our meetings, we also shared the information we were getting from the outside.

Barbed wire fences lined the prison camp, yet that didn't keep away young believers who would whisper words of encouragement or sing to us through the wire, bringing a bit of brightness into our dark days.

Our work at that camp was to weave basket bags of nylon threads called *avoska* (literally "maybe" or "just in case"). People carried such bags with them "in case" they found a bargain somewhere. The threads were tangled in big balls, and everybody scrambled to pull out as much thread as possible. You had to have enough thread to fulfill your daily quota—or else. Our fingers were rubbed raw from weaving and our hands were cut to the bones, but we had no choice and no one to complain to. Those who went to the doctor with bloody hands had their daily quota increased and their food intake decreased. There was never enough thread, of course, making it impossible by design to fulfill our quotas.

Yasha got a better work detail in the prison kitchen, eventually rising to head cook. For my birthday on December 15, he wanted to surprise me with some fried potatoes. But the superintendent caught him, and he was put into the isolation cell for ten days. He paid dearly for a present I didn't even receive, but Yasha had no regrets.

No one inside the prison could believe at first that Yasha had become a believer. Everyone was scared of him for his temper and his nasty reputation, as both a brute and an outlaw, initiating gambling and the drinking of *chifir* (an extremely strong tea used as a drug).

They thought "his roof had moved aside" and he had gone crazy. But Yasha was of sound mind, a new man, inside and out.

The operational department and an officer named Chernetsov in particular were outraged that I had led Yasha to Christ. He would call me in to his office where he would yell and curse and smack me in the face over and over. "I give you my word as a KGB officer—I will let you rot in this place!"

Soon after his conversion, Yasha was sent to another prison, separated from me but not from God. We were lifelong friends, and Yasha's wife and children also came to serve the Lord.

8

Ermakov Island

TRULY, THE CONDITIONS AT THE PRISON camp on Ermakov Island were barbaric, designed to exterminate prisoners who could not be "rehabilitated." The island was three miles wide and five and a half miles long. In the fifth century, Greeks sailing by the island would sail into the mouth of the Danube River to trade in Vilkovo. Then as now, the island was a freezing, muddy swampland, full of starvation, exhaustion, and backbreaking labor. Many times I was boosted by the example of John, who wrote Revelation in unbearable conditions on Patmos, also an island prison, located in the Aegean Sea.

In the winter, an icy wind would blow through the holes and cracks in the barrack walls, chilling us to the bone.

The Danube River was a natural border with Romania. From the opposite bank of the river we could hear the cries and curses of Romanian prisoners. Who knows? Maybe their conditions were even worse than ours.

There were no letters allowed on the island, which may have been the hardest thing of all.

Every morning, in any season, we walked a couple miles to our work detail: mowing down the reedy overgrowth. In summer, spring, and fall, we worked in standing water, often up to our waists. As winter came, and the water froze over, the ice would sometimes crack and we would plunge into the frigid water. Some prisoners died this way. Our arms and legs would go numb with cold, yet we were not allowed near the fire, which was for the prison guards only.

In warmer weather, there was the danger of quicksand in the marshes. One day, two prisoners fell into the hole, and when others tried to save them they were sucked in as well.

When it rained, a thick, oozing mud would cover every surface, and my boots felt as if they weighed two hundred pounds with each step. The convoy drivers, often drunk and belligerent, would become angry at any slowdown whatsoever, and would set their snarling dogs on us.

The guards had lots of fun at our expense, sometimes ordering us to lie down in the mud as they shot off a round of bullets right over our heads. Once, two prisoners got shot and died, but the officers were let off without even a slap on the wrist.

One day, a prisoner, who had gotten a parcel from relatives, treated me to a piece of lard. I was going to savor it, grilling it in a small fire in the reeds. I could hardly wait to taste this piece of heaven! But when I picked it up off the grill, I dropped it into the water and a muskrat snatched it and swam away. Oh, what a disappointment! After endless days with barely enough food to survive, I watched in disbelief as my precious treasure swam away down the river. Muskrats were hunted by the prisoners and eaten raw, their skins used to line boots, if someone was lucky enough to have boots.

Once, when we had heavy rains, the roofs started leaking badly and our bedding got soaked, which caused worms to infiltrate our pillows, mattresses and clothes. Some of the prisoners, desperate to leave and go to the "dry prison" in Vilkovo, injected themselves with sulfur, which would cause terrible swelling of the limbs. It was a huge risk; some prisoners died or had to have their arms and legs amputated. Those who survived were transported to the hospital in Vilkovo. They were the lucky ones who managed to get out of there.

Sometimes, I wondered if I would survive at all. But just when I thought I couldn't bear it anymore, my Christian brothers and sisters from the church in Shevchenkovo came to help. They arrived at the island with great difficulty, despite ice floes and other dangers, and somehow persuaded the director of the camp to let me wear the warm sheepskin coat they had brought along. On another visit, one of the brothers convinced an officer to sneak me a pair of sturdy, waterproof boots. That coat and those boots saved my life many times. Several times we were allowed to visit face to face through a wire fence, which was an oasis in the "desert" to me. When they die and go to heaven, I know God will commend them for their compassion. "I was in prison, and you came to me" (Matt. 25:36).

Christ's Hands

Illness was no excuse to miss work. A doctor, a volunteer whom we called "Vulture," gave very few notes to excuse prisoners from their work. A visit to this "healer" would go like this:

"What is your problem?"

"I have a fever and I'm feeling dizzy . . ."

"Lift your hands! Wave your hands! And now, little bird, fly to mow down more weeds!"

One day, I was so sick with a high temperature I couldn't get out of bed. After the roll call, the warden, accompanied by three officers, entered my barrack. The warden sneered at me. "Ah, God-Prayer, why are you lying here? Don't you know you are supposed to get a release from the doctor?"

He ordered the officers to lift me out of bed and throw me in a pool of ice cold water on the ground. They trampled me with their boots, laughing and mocking me. "We shall not let you leave this island alive! We are used to prisoners much tougher than you and we always break them!"

My nose was broken and my lip was split open. Blood ran down my face as I lay there in shivering in the icy water, unable to get up. "Lord! You see me here. Give me strength to forgive my offenders. I am asking in the name of Your blood: heal me. Whatever my sufferings, give me health."

That very moment, I felt Jesus bending over me. Warmth filled my body, and even the muddy water became warmer. "Don't be afraid, for I am with you," he said to me, bracing me as I got on my feet.

I was healed, body and soul. My nose was fixed, my fever gone, and my legs that had hurt since my childhood were pain free. I ran out of the barracks, and the guard on duty looked at me with wide eyes. "What happened to you? A few minutes ago you were unable to get up, and now you are running!"

"Can't you see? God has healed me!" I shouted, full of joy. He was speechless.

Jesus had come to me on my own Patmos Island, laying his healing touch on my body and restoring my health. My faith grew like a reed on the marsh that day and in the days to come.

Even in my cold, wet solitary confinement cell (my punishment for not working), I sang out to God. Through a small window high above my head I watched the dawn, and through the night I talked to my best friend, my Lord, thanking him.

A no-nonsense guard took me out of my cell the next day. "Why are you happy?" he asked, confused.

"How can I help not being happy after the Lord had healed me? I am praying for you, too, for all the prisoners, for all of us."

What was going through his mind? I can only imagine. That tough guard was kinder to me from that day on. He had witnessed a miracle, and he couldn't deny it.

9

A New Prison

AT THE END OF 1964, I was transported to a new camp on the mainland, near the banks of the Dnieper River, where unfortunately reeds also grew in abundance. But there was a saving grace: young believers from Odessa would come and sing outside the barbed wire fence, their voices like angels filtering through the swearing, filth, and godlessness. The KGB of course wanted to know who these people were and where they were from.

I once passed a letter to my friend Stephen through a voluntary worker. I asked him to meet me at a spot on the river where I would be mowing reeds. I drew him a map, and urged him to come early in the morning, before the guards would be on patrol.

Two young believers, Tamara and Anna, decided to disguise themselves as men, wearing *ushanka* hats, padded coats, men's pants, and fishermen's boots, so they could come along with Stephen. They put together a care package with food, letters, clothes and some books, and in the middle of the night another friend drove the three to the appointed spot.

I waited anxiously in the reeds, silently praying they would find me and not be caught. Suddenly, I heard steps, and to my great relief it was Stephen, Tamara, and Anna. Together we crawled further into the reeds, looking for a more sheltered spot to have our meeting. We talked and ate together as long as we could possibly risk it, and then I said good-bye to them, grieved at our parting but encouraged also.

A prison mate whom I trusted hid the contents of the care package in a spare pair of boots he had each brought. Every single morsel and word on a page meant the world to me, and I cherished it all.

"Father Leonid"

I had a friend named Leonid inside the prison who had once been a respected captain in the navy. He had been discharged, and sentenced to five years in prison and five in exile for openly confessing his faith, leaving the Communist Party, and preaching to military officers.

Cheerful and friendly, Leonid had never lost his sense of humor, even in that sinkhole of a place. He was well known in prison as an educated man and a teacher of the Bible. The other prisoners called him Father Leonid. He was often shut up in solitary confinement, as you can imagine.

On one occasion, USSR leader Nikita Khrushchev was coming to our city to take part in some celebrations, and the city was preparing itself to welcome the dear visitor. The KGB was taking every precaution to ensure no one would revolt or cause trouble, so the most dangerous criminals were to be isolated in solitary confinement during Khrushchev's visit. The KGB colonel and the major of the Ministry of Internal Affairs arrived at camp to manage all the precautionary measures.

Leonid and I, as "dangerous criminals," were called to the director's office to meet with these officials. Leonid was announced by name and sentence, and suddenly began making the sign of the cross on both officials. "I am giving you the sign of the cross, you officers of the devil!" Of course, he mocked them with his blessing.

Their faces registered shock, and then fury. Sparks were shooting out of their eyes and they looked as if they might combust. "Do you *know* who is arriving in our city?" They managed to sputter.

"I know," Leonid replied in a lilting fashion, "The chief demon of the CPSU!" In Russian, the words came out like a nursery rhyme.

I burst out laughing—I couldn't help it. The director of the camp, red in the face, rose from his seat and shouted at us. "Fifteen days in an isolation ward for you! And for you, Bondarenko, ten days for your participation! Take them away!"

And thus for Leonid and I, Khrushchev's visit was especially solemn as we welcomed our dear leader from the underground solitary confinement cells of the prison camp. The story of Leonid's brash blessing spread like wildfire through the prison as delighted prisoners repeated it over and over. From then on, the term "Father Leonid" was met with a chuckle for years to come.

One more story illustrates Father Leonid's beloved stature in the prison. We and the other prisoners were lined up to go to work detail one morning, when a couple of prisoners challenged us:

"You and Bondarenko—You say God is almighty, so can you pray and ask your "almighty" God to give us so much rain today we can stay in our barracks and get out of work?" A day off of work in prison was a miracle on the level of Moses parting the Red Sea.

I noted nervously that the sky was blue without a single cloud.

But Leonid and I got down on our knees right there, joined by Vladimir, another believer condemned for his faith. Everybody fell silent as we prayed, earnestly praying to God to work his wonders before our skeptical friends.

We waited in faith, and about twenty minutes later we got our miracle: the blue sky suddenly turned black with dark clouds. When the convoy arrived to take us to work, a heavy rain began to pound down on us all. It was decided that, due to this severe rainstorm, we would spent the day in the barracks instead of working. What a celebration erupted the minute the officials made that call. Everybody was shouting and jumping up and down. "God exists! He really does!"

Meeting My Parents

It was in that prison camp that an even greater miracle occurred: In that camp God gave me a present: I was allowed to see my parents face to face. How the anticipation built for that blessed day! But the time finally came, and brought every comfort I had longed for. With tears of joy streaming down our faces, we hugged and kissed each other with profound emotion.

My mother's eyes were also filled with pain at the sight of her son, pale, weak, and sickly thin. She stroked my head with her hands, and cried again, this time because her heart was broken.

My mother took white bread, homemade sausages, pies, cheeses, and honey out of her bag. I could hardly believe I was going to be able to partake of these delicious foods, which smelled better than anything in the whole world—they smelled like *home*.

We talked of the growing church in our country, of revival and passionate service. I felt like I was on an island of security and warmth in a sea of danger and suffering. The words "The meeting is over. Go out!" cut me like a knife. We slowly collected our things, and committed one another to God's keeping, parting with grief in our hearts. The look in my mother's eyes as she left stayed with me for a long time to come. Little did I know, this visit was to bolster me and keep me sane in the torment that was just around the corner.

❊ ❊ ❊

The next prison to which I was transported was to be my last, but I didn't know that at the time. They classified me as a "CI," which meant I was to be transported in complete isolation. I was considered dangerous to be around, even for criminals. One notation in my file said this: "He is able to convert anybody to his faith by means of agitation."

Transport in summer was unbearable; the sweltering heat, the cell-like carriages, like cages at a zoo. Once a day we were taken out to go to the toilet; otherwise we had to use our boots as toilets.

I was given rotten herring and two rations of bread a day. Water was rare, and my lips were stuck together because of my extreme thirst. Other prisoners in the convoy turned into animals, screaming wildly for water. It was unendurable, our existences completely focused on one sip of water.

On my third day at the new prison, I was taken to an office where KGB officers waited for me. They accused me of forcing my cellmates to accept faith in Christ, and forcibly put me in a straitjacket, a prisoner's worst nightmare.

A straitjacket is made of material that shrinks when it is wet. It is laced up in the front, and the long sleeves are tied behind the back. The officers doused me with ice cold water, and with terrifying speed the jacket shrunk, and I felt like I was being squeezed to death. Surely, my bones would break! I moaned and screamed in agony. When I passed out, they revived me with liquid ammonia, and began dousing me all over again.

"Why are you putting up with this?" My torturers were enjoying themselves. "We'll stop at once—just renounce your God!" The rule was that this kind of torture couldn't last for more than two hours at one time, so finally, blissfully, it ended. But after a few hours, they began again, and then again, for fifteen days and nights. If I was conscious, I prayed to God to rescue me.

His answer came in the form of a prison inspector, who made unannounced visits to monitor the way inmates were being treated. Seeing my wretched condition, I was brought to a prison hospital where I was treated for two weeks.

After my hospitalization, I was barely on the doorway of my new barrack when a man rushed towards me in a flurry. "I know who you are—you are God's man!" His mouth was foaming, and his eyes were burning with hatred. "I will kill you right here! I hate you people, you saints," he waved his fist menacingly. "You are not the first saint I've killed. I already sent my wife to paradise!"

I was stunned at first. *What in the world?* Then I realized an evil spirit had taken control of this man. "By the name of the Lord Jesus Christ," I spoke with authority, "I command you to stay away from me!"

He stepped back, but went on shouting and waving his hands and then fell down on the floor convulsing. Everybody watched with shock and horror. God demonstrated that by His name His children could oppose the power of the enemy. The other prisoners regarded me with wide eyes. I was immediately given a bed in a good spot by the window.

For three months, I worked in a paint shop, choking on paint fumes in an airless shop. But it was here where God would grant me reprieve like he did with his servant Joseph, Jacob's son.

One day I was called away from work rather urgently by the director of the camp. Someone with my engineering skills was needed to replace a prisoner working in the technical department who had been released on amnesty. Without him the factory would not fulfill its quota, and they were desperate enough that the director overrode the KGB's protests. "We are not talking about his ideology at the moment, but rather about his professional skills," he said.

Everything about this appointment was an improvement, including my supervisor, a decent man who appreciated my skill and the way I helped others with their jobs as well. He was curious about me, and perplexed. Did I really believe in God? To him, as to many others, my faith seemed to be a strange thing. But to me, there was nothing so valuable and precious.

10

The First Release

AFTER A FEW MONTHS of working in the prison factory's technical department, I heard that Father Leonid and another believer friend of mine had been released. I wondered about God's vision to me in the Odessa prison. The three-year mark was approaching, and I believed freedom was coming. Of course, when I shared this with my co-workers they thought I was crazy.

One morning, I felt sure this would be the day of my release. My cellmates laughed long and loud when I told them this, but I knew it was true.

Normally, if someone was going to be released, they were released at 11 a.m. When nothing happened by about ten minutes to noon, I began to lose hope, despite myself. Then I noticed three little birds, beautiful and rare, knocking at my window with their beaks. The first, the second, the third, and then they flew away. "Look," I said to my cellmates, "three knocks, like my three years in prison..."

At noon the door opened, and the director of the camp came

in, accompanied by the officer on duty and the leader of the brigade. "Prisoner Bondareko, according to the verdict of the Odessa regional court, you have been released because of lack of corpus delicti. You have been rehabilitated. Take your things, get your dismissal papers, and go to the prison checkpoint."

Everyone's jaws dropped open. My prison mates were so happy that they grabbed me and threw me in the air. "God exists! You have been telling us the truth. It's a miracle!"

I gathered my things and began to say good-bye. Everybody was congratulating me. My friends from my barrack and work came, and I prayed for them to be released soon, too.

I bid everyone farewell, and felt sorry for them all as I walked toward the prison checkpoint. These inmates needed compassion and understanding.

Nobody searched me and nobody tried to stop me. Only the officer who was in charge of fulfilling prison regulations said something. "Your release is spittle in the face of the Soviets," he said, not looking me in the eye. "You have proved to be right about your God."

The first door opened, the second one, and the third one—I was a free man. Only someone who knows that bondage, of barbed wire and the bared teeth of guard dogs and overseers, can understand this feeling of freedom. The sun itself seemed to shine more brightly and warmly that day.

No one knew about my release, so I walked alone out of camp, dressed in a prisoner's uniform. I couldn't believe I was walking somewhere by myself; no guards with machine guns followed me. The moment I had longed for had finally come, and now I was free to do whatever I wanted. I hopped a bus to take me to the closest church I could find, which was in a nearby village.

※ ※ ※

In 1965, many prisoners, including leading ministers of the persecuted church, were released. Prayers of believers in the Soviet

Union and around the world facilitated our release. Nikolai was also released, and it was a time of precious homecomings, reunions, and celebrations.

My welcome in Odessa was especially wondrous. My brothers and sisters carried me to the pulpit to give my testimony. Nikolai and I were the first prisoners of that church, which was packed out with rejoicing believers, anxious to hear our stories.

I wanted to visit friends in all the churches that prayed for me, but first things first: it was time to go home to my family in Kapitanovka.

My mother ran out to welcome me. She had aged even since her visit to me in prison, but her face was shining. "Joseph! Praise the Lord, you are alive! It's not a dream anymore!" My dad ran out and we all embraced each other in the yard. Many neighbors and friends came to greet me, and our whole community celebrated.

It was spring, the air was getting warmer and the birds were singing. That night, I couldn't fall asleep because I was so excited. A nightingale sang somewhere in the night, and the song seemed to be a tribute to my freedom.

In the morning and every morning after, my mom gave me fresh milk to regain my strength. My brothers and sisters came to our home to rejoice over my return, and it was like the happy days of our childhood again, working together, cooking, eating, and clearing the table. One evening, we talked about my plans for the future, and the brave among my family members told me now it was time for me to get married.

On my first emotional Sunday home, I went to the church in which I had grown up. Here I felt the spirit of the early Christians, surrounded with simple-hearted, noble-minded people who sincerely loved the Lord.

When I think of that period, it was much like the time of Esther and Mordecai: "In each and every province and in each and every city . . . there was gladness and joy . . . a feast and a holiday" (Est. 8:17). How could I stop thanking God that He had kept me safe and given me my freedom again?

In the Presence of Mine Enemies

On a sunny August morning in 1965, I helped lead a youth rally in a big park in Lviv. Of course, this was an extremely risky and dangerous course of action. By 10 a.m. hundreds of believers from different churches in the area gathered in that beautiful park, eager to worship together and hear solid Bible teaching.

The city authorities were on high alert. People said they had never seen so many militiamen in their city; it looked like some kind of overthrow was planned. On street corners and crossings there were cars and motorbikes driven by militiamen and KGB officers. The city authorities did their best to disturb our service. Citizens, encouraged to drink heavily, were loud and unruly, and motorbikes without mufflers drove past the park, back and forth. It was nearly impossible to hear our rally.

The situation became very heated. Some KGB officers pushed their way through the crowd, and one of them, wielding a knife, came rushing towards me but the crowd got in his way. I quickly prayed for wisdom, and God instructed me to get everybody down on their knees on the wet grass to pray. Down on the ground, we could easily see who the KGB officers were (they were the ones standing). Hundreds of believers closed ranks around me and the KGB were unable to seize me.

The service went on. The Word of God was preached, a Christian brass band and choir performed. The more the authorities tried to disrupt the service, the more the people in the park wanted to listen to us. But the confrontations were becoming too violent and something had to give. Then I had an idea. "If you go on disturbing our fellowship," I announced, "we will be obliged to move to the central square of the city to continue the program there." It worked. The KGB and friends immediately cooled it, and we were able to continue, uninterrupted.

When the service ended, the question became how I would escape the KGB officers, who were waiting to seize me. We decided on safety in numbers. Together, we would walk to the tram terminal and squeeze in as many as possible. Safely onboard, we found out the tram was now going to make an unscheduled stop, right by the KGB office where they would be ready to seize me. Another quick prayer and a split second decision: Everyone would get off at the KGB stop, except for me and a few friends. I disguised myself with a new coat, hat and glasses someone loaned me. When the large group of believers got off at the stop, I watched as militiamen rushed towards them, trying to find me. It had not occurred to the KGB that we would dare go further in an almost empty tram.

We got off at the next stop, and my friend Peter, who knew the city well, navigated us through that neighborhood and out of the city. We waited at a certain spot outside the city, until a bus full of our Christian friends stopped by and picked us up.

This wasn't the first or last time the KGB was thwarted in its attempts to arrest me again. Through many rallies and services all over the Soviet Union—Siberia, Ukraine, Belarus, Moldova, Russia—God concealed me over and over again "in the presence of my enemies" (Ps. 23:5).

It was at one of these events, a church visit in Brest, Belarus, that my world turned upside down—in a good way. I was twenty-nine and so busy with the work of the Lord, I hadn't had time to devote to thinking about marriage, let alone even looking for the right young lady. But God saw me in my confusion, and brought the perfect woman right to me.

I'll never forget that blessed night. My friend Vladimir and I were leading a youth service in a private home, and as usual, after the meeting, I spent some time meeting those in attendance. One of these young people was the enchanting Maria Pinkevich. She approached me shyly and smiled. "My name is Maria," she said. As I held her hand, my heart began to pound in a way it never had. My head felt a little dizzy, and I was shocked at my response to her. Sure, I had felt a connection to other girls in the past, but nothing prepared me for the thrill I had holding Maria's hand. She was beautiful, but I could also sense in her a quiet depth of character, intelligence, and good sense. Yes—I could sense all those things in one handshake! I wanted to stay and talk to this mysterious creature, but alas, it was not to be. My friends were rushing me out of the house, as it was time to go. We had to leave for another town that very night.

A Delegation to Moscow

In the autumn of 1965, more than a hundred believers, including ex-prisoners from various churches and areas, arrived in Moscow to try and negotiate the release of those who had been imprisoned for their faith. This delegation wanted a meeting with Anastas Mikoyan, an old-time Bolshevik and member of the Politburo, the executive committee and highest governing body for the Central Committee of the Communist Party of the Soviet Union. With the fall of Khrushchev in 1964, Mikoyan was a top policymaker as well as the nominal head of state.

We camped out for a week at his office, fasting and singing songs, despite the numerous threats we received.

Our argument was that these prisoners had been condemned according to charges in articles 227 and 229 of the criminal code, which covered drunkenness, acts of perversion, keepers of various illegal bars, and so on. We requested the authorities reconsider the sentences, as this code was inapplicable to the believers' actions.

To say the least, they were not happy to have us there, pleading our case. At the end of the workday, the door and windows of the waiting room were closed, and then suddenly about thirty militiamen started throwing punches and shoving and kicking us. After beating us until we were bloody and our clothes were torn, they demanded we go home or be arrested.

Despite all the threats, we came again the next day and demanded to see Mikoyan. We made up our minds to not leave until our petition was heard. Finally, later that day, accompanied by a militia detachment, Rudenko, the general public prosecutor, came in the waiting room and addressed us: "Why are you seeking an audience with the government?"

We made our demands: the release of our brothers and sisters, languishing in prisons and camps on trumped-up charges; the return to believers of their church buildings, and in some cases, their very children, who had been taken away because of their parents' beliefs.

Rudenko listened and replied that it was out of his hands and we should appeal to the Politburo. "And now, please, leave the waiting room."

"Dear Mr. Rudenko," I said, "Thank you for coming, but if you can't help us, we shall pray again, asking God to open the hearts of the government so that they pay attention to the sufferings of His people."

All the delegates dropped to our knees in prayer, which caused Rudenko to panic, thinking we were asking God to curse him. "Do not curse me—it's not my fault!" he pleaded loudly. "I am not guilty, please, do not curse me!"

Suddenly his fear cooled and was replaced by anger. "Bondarenko," he said, "I'll get you for this!" He and his minions turned on their heels and left the room.

We were still praying and fasting late the next day when Mikoyan's representative came to the waiting room and told us we had been given an audience with the leader on September 22, with one condition: only five of us would be allowed the audience.

Carrying all the official documents concerning the persecution of believers, the five who were chosen—myself, Baturin, Yakimenko, Kozlov, and Govorun (who was also a member of the Council of Prisoners' Relatives)—showed up that day in the Presidium, where we were led into the Kremlin. Members of the Kremlin staff stared at us as though we were cavemen. "Sectarians inside the Kremlin! Who has let them in?"

We were invited to enter a private office on the third floor. The interior was luxurious, with expensive furniture, soft carpets on the floor, paintings in beautiful frames, and opulent curtains on the windows.

Six men were sitting in comfortable armchairs: Mikoyan, Malyarov, the deputy general, Puzin, the chairman in charge of religious cults, two more officials, and a KGB officer. We were given less than an hour.

Baturin thanked them for their time, and began to state our case. He showed documents and pictures proving a martyr's death, how houses of prayer had been seized, and children taken away from their believing parents. Arrests of believers, he said, were on-going, as they were taken into custody for preaching the gospel.

Mikoyan objected, saying these injustices had taken place in the past. We presented him with proof, pictures of houses of prayer being destroyed in pogroms, and more than thirty documents, confirming new and current persecutions.

Mikoyan told us they would carefully look over everything and give us their answer, yet it was clear they had only glanced at a third of the documents. "Mr. Mikoyan," I said, "our delegation was beaten right here, in the waiting room of the Presidium. Can you imagine what is happening in the provinces, where officials are not closely monitored? Please consider our case!"

At one point, Mikoyan interrupted me and said he knew first-hand that believers were honest and good workers. He had worked with them himself in the1920s, in Rostov. He acknowledged that the persecutions we had described were against the law, and prom-ised to address the matter himself, creating a more lawful relation-ship between the state and believers.

However, after a month had passed, Anastas Mikoyan retired to his summer home, and his promises to us went unfulfilled.

The Second Attempt

The year 1966 brought nothing but a new wave of persecutions, so Georgi Vins and I decided to initiate and organize a second del-egation to Moscow in the middle of May. Vins was a good friend and a well-known Russian pastor and a dissident who was greatly persecuted by the Soviet government for his boldness in preaching the gospel and was later expelled from the Soviet Union. It was a carefully planned and strategically executed plan to protect reli-gious rights. This time, we wanted to obtain an audience with the

General Secretary of the Central Committee, Leonid Brezhnev, or the members of the Politburo.

When we were refused an audience with Brezhnev, some of the delegates spent the night on the streets, while the rest of us stayed in believers' homes, waiting for word of what to do next.

I secretly met with Vera Shuportyak, one of the delegates, in a park not far from the building of the Central Committee. We had little time as we noticed immediately we were being spied on, so Vera quickly whispered the bad news: the members of the delegation had been beaten badly and arrested.

The spies were closing in on us, so Vera and I began running. Miraculously, we caught a taxi and eluded them. I had a feeling we could trust the cab driver and I told him we were believers, most likely being pursued at that moment by the KGB. He put his foot on the gas pedal and drove as fast as he could. "I was imprisoned in times of Stalin," he said. "I know what their 'kitchen' is like." ("Kitchen" is an idiomatic expression, referring to the KGB's tactics, such as falsifying evidence, making wrongful criminal accusations, fabricating trials, and so on.)

He was an experienced driver who knew the city well, and he helped us escape even though the secret police were in hot pursuit. Having paid the driver and thanked him, we crept through a bunch of backyards until we got to a believer's home, the secret meeting place where other brothers and sisters were waiting for news.

Despite the fact that the KGB were on high alert since our delegation had converged upon the Kremlin again, as directors of the delegation we were responsible for our people, and we had to go back and find out more about what had happened.

Though I wanted to be the one to go, Vins and Mikhail Khorev argued that they should go. (Khorev was a friend, co-worker, and Russian Baptist leader who suffered enormous persecution and several imprisonments, remaining faithful to the Lord till the end. He and I began a movement of Christian youth that rallied throughout the Soviet Union during a most difficult time for the church.) So after some back and forth, we all agreed that the two of them should go, and we prayed for their safety as they left. One, two, and then three anxious, fear-filled hours passed, and our two brothers still had not returned. There was no doubt in anyone's minds that they were never coming back.

Later we found out that the delegates who had slept in Red Square had been rounded up by militiamen with machine guns, beaten, and trampled. The sisters were dragged by their hair to busses, which were there to transport each and every delegate to prison.

Things were terribly grim. Those who remained decided I would somehow get myself from Moscow to Kiev, where I would report what had happened to the believers there and spread it to brothers and sisters all over the country.

But how could I get out of the capital? All the airports, train stations, and roads were being monitored and documents inspected closely. I prayed for wisdom and felt God prompting me to take a bus to the outskirts of Moscow, where I then pretended to be a worker on the garbage truck I saw. Thus I was able to slip out of Moscow, and arrived in Kiev by noon the next day, where I immediately contacted some leaders of the local church.

Sister Vasyanova hosted us all in her apartment, where we collaborated on a message to inform all the believers of the cruel treatment and arrests in Moscow. Copies were to be made and distributed to all the churches. I had plans to go to Riga, Latvia, to manage the affairs of the persecuted church there.

But I had an uneasy feeling, wondering if I would ever get the chance. I had spied a Volga parked near the sister's apartment, and it seemed suspicious to me that there were men sitting and talking inside the car. Sure enough, within moments, officers of the KGB burst into the apartment.

I quickly ripped the message to the believers into pieces and was swallowing it, but an officer rushed over to me, grabbed me by the throat and clawed at my mouth, trying to retrieve any pieces I had not swallowed. The officers twisted mine and another brother's arms painfully behind our backs, and began to interrogate us. "Where are the others who had organized the delegation? Where is

Kryuchkov?" Gennadi Kryuchkov was chairman of the Council of Churches and a well-known Baptist leader who served three years of imprisonment and for many years went underground.

We kept silent, and soon the apartment was encircled by KGB vehicles. People who gathered on the street to stare were told American spies with a radio transmitter had been caught. They took our passports and my railway ticket for Riga. We were both arrested and taken into custody. It was May 1966, and I was a captive man once again.

11

The Second Imprisonment: 1966–69

THIS IS HOW I FOUND myself in a Kiev prison, whose main building was a four-storied stone structure with high ceilings, long corridors, and steep steps made of worn stone. It was built in the eighteenth century, in the times of Russian tsarina Catherine II. There was a room in the prison that used to be a prison church, but hadn't been used as a place of worship for years.

There were five to six thousand prisoners being housed there when I arrived.

The basement fascinated me, with its numerous underground passages connecting different parts of the prison. In some places they came together, in some places they branched off. It was a complicated and intricate system.

I was put into a cell with about fifty other prisoners, thieves of all kinds, and many repeat offenders. Older, hardened criminals ruled everyone else, presiding as masters over pickpockets, racketeers, and drug dealers and addicts. They took for themselves the best beds, with the most access to air and light.

Then there were the "Brood Hens," or whistleblowers to prison management. You wanted to steer clear of them because they would turn in their own grandmothers for an "infraction."

Each prisoner was either given a "residence permit" through a kind of hazing ritual that went on for newcomers, or they weren't given one, in which case they were outcasts and spit upon by their fellow inmates.

I entered the cell, greeted everyone and went to lay my duffle bag down on my bed, right next to the smelly *parasha*. I knelt down and prayed by my bed, and when I opened my eyes a huge guy with a square face and a wide scar on his forehead came up and began asking me questions. I told him I was a believer.

"Don't you know Christ?" I asked. "What about the tattoo on your chest, of the crucified Christ?"

"This is a holy thing," he said about his tattoo. "We speak only good about Him here, between ourselves. What charges did they make up about you anyway? The cops are all against us here, too."

Everyone in the "hut," or group, nodded in agreement.

"I see you are here all by yourself," the tattooed man said. "Come, move your bed away from the *parasha* and come over here by us. We like saints here."

He told me about the rules and order in this "hut," and how even though thieves had different rules and order, this group was on friendly terms with them. "Join our family here," he invited, "We need your prayers!"

This was how I got my "residence permit" without any of the misery they usually inflict on newcomers. The huge guy whispered something to the inmate currently sitting on a bed under the window, and he jumped up and gave his bed to me.

I spent twenty days in that cell, before my witnessing got me thrown into a "T-bend," a damp and cold three-cornered solitary cell with not even a mattress to sleep on.

One night I woke up with a start. The iron door rattled, and suddenly two jailers came inside, pushing a muscular young man covered in blood, his scalp just hanging off his head. I sprang up from the floor as chills went up and down my spine. I knew at once he was clearly demon possessed. The young man rushed at me, striking the air with his fists and threatening to kill me. "By the name of the Lord Jesus Christ I forbid you to touch me!" I commanded. "Lord! Save me from this terrible demon!"

He stepped back and went on screaming and waving his fists, with blood dripping and flying everywhere. Over and over again I prohibited him from hurting me by the name of the Lord. This went on for several hours, until suddenly the door opened and he was taken away. Immediately the whole cell was lighter, and my relief overwhelmed me.

When I tried to report what had happened to the prison management, they acted as if nothing had happened and that young man had never been in my cell. Once more I came to understand that there was nobody to complain to. Almighty God was my only hope.

Many times throughout my imprisonment I was called in for interrogation by the KGB, who hoped to get the names and locations of other believers and churches.

At one point, the KGB promised to set me free in exchange for my agreement to cooperate with them and give them information. When I flatly refused, they didn't take it well. "Looks like you want to destroy your life completely," they snarled at me. "You'll be sorry for this."

The next weeks, months and years would turn out to be some of the most painful and difficult of my life, but yet I never regretted my decision. I cherished my freedom in Christ a thousand times more than the freedom the KGB had offered me.

Cell 105

I will remember my next cell block for the rest of my life. Cell 105 was designed for twenty prisoners, but there were sixty of them stuffed inside those dirty cement walls. It stank horribly in there, of unwashed bodies, the overflowing *parasha*, and the nonstop haze of cigarette smoke, which burned my eyes night and day. The tight squeeze made everyone a little crazy, and sometimes the other prisoners argued and fought like caged animals.

There were twenty rules hanging on the wall, so no one could forget for a minute. We had to "decorate" our cells with traditional red on certain holidays and take out excrement twice a day. We were forbidden to sit by the door, approach the window, write notes in books, sing, or communicate with knocks. If we disobeyed in the slightest, our "privileges" would be revoked and we might even have to be put in solitary confinement.

After a while, my cellmates began to trust me and ask me questions about the innocent One who had suffered deeply and was able to understand anyone who suffered, including them. Who created the world? What would the end of the world be like? I answered every question to the best of my ability.

My cellmates even liked it when I told them Bible stories and read from books I borrowed from the prison library. They enjoyed these stories so much I could even get them to quit smoking while I was narrating!

One day some of the prisoners and I made up our minds to learn John 3:16 by heart: "For God so loved the world . . ." My cellmates even gave me a place in the corner of the cell to pray. Nobody was allowed to even step on that holy spot. As I was praying, my cellmates hushed. "Keep silent," they would whisper, "the saint is praying!"

Of course, the prison authorities got wind of this, and my cellmates were scattered to different cells while I was thrown into the dreaded punishment cell. For fifteen days, I was not allowed my daily walk and never had one breath of fresh air. Some of the prisoners did not come out of this punishment with their sanity intact, and some days I felt like I was also losing my grip.

Thoughts that I had been forgotten by everyone invaded my heart and soul. I felt even my parents had forsaken me as I sat in that bone-chilling, claustrophobic cell, day after day. How could I endure this?

The "Trial"

When I returned to the community cell, I met a new fellow prisoner named Izya, a young man who had been imprisoned for his participation in a famous crime: the murder of a female cashier at the "Bolshevik" factory in Kiev.

The murder victim had been a friend of Izya's family. Her job was to pick up and transport large sums of money from the bank to the factory in an armored car. On the day of the murder, the actual killer, Yaroslavskiy, had his fiancée call the cashier and, using the name of her boss, tell her the armored car would not arrive in time. She advised her to catch a passing car.

Meanwhile, Yaroslavskiy asked for Izya's permission to use his car, not telling him what he wanted it for. Izya agreed. The plan was quite simple: Yaroslavskiy and his companion would be passing by the bank, and the cashier would ask them to give her a lift to the factory. They murdered her in the car, and took the bag of money, hiding part of it in a nearby park. Yaroslavskiy thought he and his fiancée could escape to the south, but he was soon caught and arrested.

As the owner of the car, Izya was also arrested as an accessory to the crime. So he found himself in our cell. He was the only one who did not listen to me talk about God, or kneel for prayer as a group. The top dog in the cell ordered the others to beat Izya for not participating, despite my vehement protests. Izya refused to say he believed in God, no matter how many times he was beaten.

To stop the beatings, a decision was made to arrange a kind of trial, right there in the cell. A judge, prosecutor, defense attorney, and jurors were elected from amongst the prisoners. I was chosen to defend poor Izya. As I presented my case, I mentioned many passages from the Scriptures about mercy and forgiveness, and told the story of the Good Samaritan. The "trial" got everyone's attention, including the guards who came and listened to the verdict given on the last day.

Izya was released from "custody," although he could not speak out against God, neither did he have to say he believed in him. The trial was a great diversion for us all, including the guards.

The Second Verdict

On September 21, 1966, the KGB handed down their second verdict against me, sentencing me to three years of "deprivation of freedom" in a high-security prison. Several of my fellow believers were also sentenced to prison, including Nikolai Velichko, Pavel Overchuk, Andre Kechik, and Vasily Zhurilo.

Though the sentencing itself is a blur to me, some of my friends and loved ones were there to support me and pray for me, and they have a clearer memory of the day than I do. My friend Grigory recorded his memories in a notebook:

"I remember some of the peculiarities of the prisoners' behavior. Pavel looked very focused, staring intently at his document case papers without looking up even once. Nikolai was using every opportunity to turn around in his seat to see his nearest and dearest sitting in the hall. And Joseph was peering out the window. I felt for him—how difficult it must have been for him to face the bonds of imprisonment and the deprivation of freedom again. He looked to me as if he was ready to dart through the window and fly away."

What I do remember with vivid detail is being taken out of the courtroom and looking in the eyes of each person I cared about, including my beloved father, Daniel, and waving good-bye to them before I was taken back to the prison in Kiev.

My brothers and I were all accused of the same crimes. We went back to prison that day with heavy hearts, knowing the separation from those we loved would be for years.

12

Behind the Barbed Wire

A MONTH AFTER THE VERDICT, my brothers and I were scattered, each taken to different prisons. Once more I rode in a *voronok*, that suffocating machine of indignity, thirst, fear, and stench. We were packed in like sardines, given a mug of water per day, and taken to the bathroom once per day.

Have patience and keep silent. Keep silent and have patience. I repeated these words over and over again to stay sane.

We arrived in Kherson late in the evening. It was drizzling outside. When we emerged from the *voronok*, we were surrounded by snarling dogs and soldiers holding machine guns. The head of the convoy made me carry a large, cumbersome sack over my shoulders. As I trudged along with my bulky load, I felt something moving inside. When I laid the sack on the ground and looked inside, I saw a frail human being, a bony man, curled up inside. I was seized with horror. What had they done to this man?

After we reached the prison, I was ordered to take this living lump of a person to an empty cell and deposit him on the ground, alone. I found out later that this man was a local villager who had been accused of a crime that had actually been committed by the public prosecutor's sons. This man had staged a hunger strike to protest his innocence and to demand his case be reviewed. Soon after I carried him in the sack, he died a martyr's death, without having proven his case. He had never been properly tried in a court. I was shocked to my core by such inhumanity of men towards other men.

For some reason, I was put into a "condemned" cell, which is meant for those facing execution. Again, my "home" was surrounded by damp, musty walls and the constant stink of the *parasha*. My bed was made of iron, with no mattress this time, and my food was inedible for all but a starving man. I could get used to all of it, even the sharp iron pieces of my bed poking me, but not the hunger. The hunger was something I could never get used to.

❄ ❄ ❄

After a month of staying in the prison in Kherson, I was transported again, this time to Daryevka, the very camp at which I had spent much of my first term.

The operational department, the prison's own "KGB," was unhappy by my return visit, to put it mildly. They brainwashed some of the prison's top dogs on the inside, convincing them that I had sacrificed children as part of my "cult." In every prison, there was a kind of justice system in place, and in every prison, anyone accused of hurting women or children would pay for their crimes again according to the vigilante system on the inside. Avenging these crimes was a sacred act of justice for them.

As soon as the iron doors shut behind me and the guards left, the other prisoners began to enact their vengeance. They stripped off my clothes and mobbed me, beating me everywhere, but especially targeting my kidneys.

Suddenly the beating stopped cold and you could hear a pin drop.

"What is this all about?" I could tell immediately this was the chief prisoner of them all, and he was shouting. "Who are you?"

"I am a Christian believer," I said, hoarsely, wiping blood out of my eyes. "I was transported here today."

"I have met saints like you before," he said, regarding me in an interested way. "They are the good guys."

"Why have you taken his things?" He demanded of the offenders. They all stared at him, silent. I soon found out his nickname was "King." "We will find everything that was taken from you and return it to you."

King told me then that those who had beaten me had not acted according to insider prison law. They had been "worked over" by the KGB, and had not waited for an "internal investigation" into who I was before jumping on me. "We'll find out who you are and how you behaved during your first time here," he said. "We have ways of finding out if you dirtied your hands with the authorities when you were here."

In a week's time, King gathered us all around him for a meeting. He had done some checking, and received a letter from a prisoner in another cell who had been there during my first term. "It's true—you're a real believer, who defends God and your mates with everything you have," he said. "The beating you took was totally against the rules we have here, and we will punish those who did this to you." He handed me some ointment he had obtained for the cuts on my face. "You have nothing to fear here anymore. When you pray, please say a prayer for us, too." Later, those who had beaten me that first day became my friends, in keeping with my own rule: just like Jesus, whenever possible I wanted to turn enemies into friends.

A Dangerous Job

The letters "RL" were stamped on my case documents, which was a very bad thing. Those letters stood for "Rough Labor," and meant I was to be given the most grueling and dangerous work to be had: beveling iron sheets. I had to insert extremely sharp chisels into the charger of the machine, which would then cut into the iron, beveling it. My whole body vibrated constantly, and the noise, in an iron building with iron walls, was beyond deafening. Of course I was given no helmet or protective eyewear.

Many prisoners would've preferred even an isolation cell to such a job. Handling the thick, heavy sheets of vibrating iron did a number on my back, and my hands became terribly swollen. Red-hot chips of iron flew all around me like arrows, burning my hands, face, and body. At the end of a horrible day, I wouldn't even have the energy to go to the canteen and get my measly bread ration; the whole word faded to one thing: sleep. Still, I couldn't lie down until 10 p.m., according to prison rules.

One day, a red-hot chip of iron flew into my eye. The pain was ferocious, and I screamed and clutched my eye helplessly. A brigade leader heard my screams and saw what had happened. He ran to tell the guard on duty to quickly obtain a pass for me to go to the residential zone and be treated at a medical center. The minutes passed like hours as my eye seemed to be on fire. Every second that passed was crucial for saving my eye, but it was a full half an hour before that pass was signed and I was transported to the medical center.

I was given first aid, but the trauma was severe, and I needed to be hospitalized. As a rule, all prisoners with serious traumas or diseases were taken to the hospital if the medical center deemed it necessary. But I was considered to be an extremely dangerous criminal, so the operational department refused to give permission for me to be hospitalized and treated. The next day an ophthalmologist was called in, and he said I would likely lose my eye, and even if I didn't, he didn't see any chance of a good outcome. My vision would be damaged in any event. I was allowed to stay in the medical unit.

Yuri, a Christian brother who would visit me during my time in prison, heard from other inmates what had happened to me. Soon my family and friends all knew about my eye injury, and they prayed without ceasing. Letters began to pour into the medical unit, expressing deep love and concern. Several young believers were ready to donate their eyes to me, if necessary. I was shocked and humbled by their willingness to sacrifice their very eyes for a fellow believer, just like that of the Galatian believers for the apostle Paul (Gal. 4:15). What a balm for my soul and my eyes!

I have no doubt it was the prayers of God's people that caused my eyes to heal and my vision to return as good as new. This was just one of the miracles that kept my heart and soul in one piece during my times of imprisonment. God is truly *Jehovah Rapha*, the God who heals.

⧓ ⧓ ⧓

One of the biggest temptations I faced was an offer made to me by someone who had the power to grant the desires of my heart. Like Satan tempting Jesus in the desert, this man knew exactly how to get under my skin. He was vice minister of internal affairs, and one day he arrived at prison camp with one purpose: to see me and remind me we had met once before under very different circumstances.

"So, Bondarenko, do you recognize me?" he asked with a sardonic smile on his face.

"No, I don't," I said, looking at him carefully.

"What if you look more closely? I'm sure you'll remember."

But I couldn't recall, no matter what. He went on. "It was near Kiev, where you were holding your big assembly. I was a police officer, and I told you to stop your preaching and your prayers. And then you said, 'Who should we listen to—you or God?'" The man had a satisfied gleam in his eye.

"Listen to me: Right now I am your "god," and the Soviet power will not let you brainwash our young people, distracting them from deeds of the happy Communist society!" He knew he was calling all the shots.

"If you don't stop spreading your fanaticism, we will put you into the cell where you will never leave until your sentence is up," he said. "But, if you give up your gibberish, you may go free tomorrow."

After sitting in the freezing cell, I felt as though this warm office was a king's palace. How I yearned to be free again! I just wanted to be treated like a human once more, to be warm, to enjoy the comfort of a family. My youth was passing me by, and I was far from all the beautiful things of life. My spirit battled within me. If I agreed to the minister's terms, I could be free!

But the Holy Spirit strengthened my will and gave me inner power to answer to him. "I will never compromise with God's enemies."

He looked surprised. "Fine, that's up to you. But know this: you will remember this meeting and the chance I gave you for a very long time."

I was taken back, but not to my cell. Instead, I was taken to a kind of outhouse, with one toilet. The air inside was a fog of disinfecting chemicals, which had no doubt been splashed everywhere with the intention of making me sick. Hour by hour passed inside that poisonous stall, until finally I passed out from the fumes.

When I wouldn't renounce my faith again the next morning, they ramped up their punishment, taking me to a solitary cell. The prison superintendent intentionally broke the glass in the barred window. It was four degrees below zero Fahrenheit outside.

Every night, they poured two or three buckets of icy water onto the floor of the cell, which meant I had to stand in the ice cold water all day. My feet stiffened, and my blood ran cold. It was a uniquely sadistic form of torture.

Anton

One day a new prisoner was thrown into the isolation cell. His name was Anton, and his whole body was covered with cuts and scars. His nose looked as if it had been broken and sewed back together a few times. Anton took one look at me and began to spew out his anger and hatred, threatening to kill me. He quickly became a bigger threat to my life than the extreme cold.

At night, I used to drop to my knees and pray, right there in the icy water. "Lord, if my death glorifies You more than my life, let Your will be done. Take me away from this horrible cell." Anton would grow even more outraged at my prayers.

I began to share my bread rations with him, although at first he wouldn't accept them. One day, he took the bread I offered him, and that day his rages weren't quite as intense. Day by day, he accepted my bread, and day by day, Anton became quieter and more subdued. It was as if I was taming a bear.

I prayed for Anton constantly, and the Holy Spirit went to work on Anton's heart. The devil had a hold on his miserable soul, but God was stronger. As I knelt down in the ice water for my evening prayers, Anton dropped to his knees beside me, praying out loud, "Lord, have mercy on me, for I am a horrible sinner. There's so much filth in my heart. Have mercy on me!"

That memorable evening, Anton accepted Jesus into his heart.

This hardened criminal and I embraced each other, and that cruel man burst into tears of joy. His face was shining. Anton had been locked up repeatedly since his childhood, he said. And in an instant he was changed forever.

"I had been put into this cell to kill you, to finally break you, but instead God broke me," he said emotionally. "They wanted to destroy you physically—with cold, hunger, ice water, and my fists, but now I will help you. Go, have your first peaceful sleep since I came."

The second the authorities figured out that their plans with Anton had backfired, they transferred him to another cell. But that was not the end of our friendship. In 1969, Anton was released and came to find me in my home village of Kapitanovka. He told me his wife and two daughters had accepted Christ. I came to his house and baptized him. Not long afterwards, Anton and his family were cherished guests of mine at one of the most special days of my life: my wedding.

13

Heart Trouble

FOR "AGITATION AND RELIGIOUS PROPAGANDA" I was moved to the PKT, or the worst of the worst cell block inside the prison, designed with great care for troublemakers, those who attempted to break out of prison, and the genuinely unrepentant, including believers.

It was within these clammy cement walls that I experienced severe chest pains, as well as numbness in my left arm. When the guards got me to a doctor, his diagnosis was firm: a small-focal myocardial infarction. He gave me an anesthetic injection and prescribed some medicine. A nurse at the medical unit watched until the guard turned away and gave me some vitamins.

The next day the same nurse gave me a piece of chocolate during an examination. I was surprised, and very much encouraged. Could she be a believer? Later I learned that the nurse and the doctor, a husband and a wife, tried to help me by all means, prescribing injections, vitamins, medicines, and lobbying the prison authorities for a more nourishing diet for me. They had come to the prison camp as part-time volunteers and were Seventh-Day Adventists.

One day, the head of the operational department was absent, and the doctor risked his job by sending me to a prison hospital in Kherson. The warden, not wanting to be responsible for my death, signed the permission slip from the prison.

Conditions at the hospital were much better. There were just eight other patients in my ward, clean sheets on my bed, and—joy of joys!—sugar and butter to stir in my morning oatmeal.

Doctor Alexander lived in Kherson, and he came to the prison hospital every day to check on me, but he couldn't actually enter the ward every time because of constant surveillance. One day, he whispered in my ear that the KGB was very anxious about my stay at the hospital. After a week, the head of the operational department returned to the prison to find me gone. He rushed to the hospital together with a KGB officer, a local public prosecutor, and the head physician of the Kherson regional hospital.

My kind guardian angel, Doctor Alexander, got to me before they did, informing me that their plan was to transport me back to the PKT or else a mental hospital nearby. The dreaded *voronok* was ready and waiting to take me to either place.

The head physician took my blood pressure, examined my lungs and my heart, and studied my medical charts. "Bondarenko's condition is critical, and I prescribe a month's stay here at the hospital for treatment," he said quietly. "In this condition, he can't be brought back to prison."

The KGB officer rushed at him, flustered. "He must go! The car is waiting, and there is a public prosecutor's signature on the papers."

The doctor was unyielding. "I am responsible for this patient's life—not you," he said. "I can't discharge him. I'm done here." He walked away, leaving the rest of the people in the room to stare at him.

After I had returned to my ward, I kneeled and thanked God, with tears of joy running down my cheeks. He had saved me once again. When I got up, I looked out the window in my ward, and I saw the black *voronok*, driving away without me.

A Visit from my Father

A month passed, and I was sent back to the prison camp from the prison hospital. My father, now seventy-four years old, came to visit me one day. "My son," he said, "if God prolongs your life and gives you freedom, I want you to get married. Pray God helps you find your faithful helpmate. Your mother and I are getting older and weaker, and, with all our hearts, we want you to have a wife who will care for you and love you unconditionally, as we do."

I began to pray with more dedication and earnestness about getting married. Did God want me to marry or to devote myself wholly to His ministry? If He did want marriage for me, who did He have in mind?

I hoped very much it was Maria, the pretty and kind young woman I had met at the meetings in Belarus. I was so very lonely in prison, and I began to think about her more and more. Marrying me would almost certainly mean suffering and hardship for her. I had already been to prison twice, and who knew what was in store for me? Could she handle it? Did she even want to try?

Imagine my excitement and joy when Maria sent me a post-card soon after I started praying dedicatedly about her. I eagerly scanned the lines of her handwriting for some clue that she also had feelings for me, but there wasn't a single hint! She expressed her Christian love, encouragement, and care, and nothing more. *She is a very cautious girl* . . . This somehow attracted me to her even more.

My sleeping hours became filled with sweet dreams of Maria, and then I would wake up to the cold reality of another day in prison. Yet thoughts of her kept me going many times.

※ ※ ※

In winter, as the river froze over, many of us were taken to a new spot to cut reeds. Under heavy guard, we were loaded into some kind of dump-truck convoy, packed so tightly it was impossible to move a muscle on our way to our new work site.

Though the guards wore fur coats, we could feel every gust of icy wind right through to our very bones. My cheeks stung from frostbite and my hands and feet had become totally numb. It was only a four-hour trip, but every minute stretched cruelly. When we arrived, none of us could stand on our frozen feet, so we were all dumped out on the ground like logs.

We stumbled painfully to our new "barrack," a barge lodged in the frozen river and surrounded by barbed wire. Inside the barge, there were bunk beds stacked three high along the walls, and so many people stuffed inside it was hard to breathe. We would wake in the night feeling panicked and suffocated, and crawl to the window and try to suck in some fresh air. It was like a gas chamber in there, airless and desperate.

At least during the day we had fresh air, but we were hungry. We used to catch fish with our bare hands and eat them raw. Two prisoners were appointed to sit by the likely spots for the fish to jump, while the rest of us worked. We shared in their daily catch, quickly getting used to raw meat.

After the backbreaking workday, we'd fall on our hard bunk beds as if dead. We didn't even have the strength to talk. But sometimes we were awoken the middle of the night by sirens, the cue that we had to go outside for inspections. They were always trying to keep us off guard and off balance, never knowing what to expect.

One Sunday a month was our day off, in which we could wash and mend our clothes, relax a little, or write a letter. This was a blessed respite from the grueling regular grind. But even on those monthly Sundays, we fell asleep thinking of bread and awoke thinking of bread.

We were allowed two trips per month to the bathhouse, where we were given a wash basin and a small piece of laundry soap. We washed ourselves on the deck of the barge, in the open air, when it was snowy and windy. But even so, to bathe at all was a great luxury. Many of prisoners caught colds on these days, but I never did. I thank my dad, who had made me and my siblings run barefoot on snow on winter evenings to get us used to cold weather.

One day we were being taken to work in the convoy, and when

we stopped. Two old women carrying bundles approached the guard. "Our Christian brother Bondarenko is here," they said, "and we want to give him some food."

"How dare you come here?" the chief guard shouted angrily. But the old women begged. "Please, have mercy, we have come such a long way!"

The guards shoved them down in the snow roughly, laughing amongst themselves. I was helpless to do anything for them, and my heart squeezed with pain. I started to protest but one of the guards hit my back with his machine gun.

The prisoners became angry with the guards. "Shame on you! Would you have done this to your mothers, your grandmothers? You are devils!" The main guard shot a few gunshots in the air, and everyone fell silent. The image of those old ladies, lying in the snow, with tears of pain rolling down their cheeks, has stayed with me, indelible, for the rest of my life.

The Second Discharge

The day I was discharged for the second time, after three years of rough labor, I remember how huge and warm and joyful the sun was, boldly shining down on me. No more were its rays obscured by prison netting or bars.

Behind the prison gates my brother Vasily and my friend Yury were waiting for me. Yury took us to his house in Kherson by car, where I was reunited with friends and fellow believers. After two days of hearty welcome and meals that nourished my body and soul, we left for the coast to meet with other believers there.

Freedom! What a dear and mysterious word! Like a bird, we were flown on the "wings" of a Rocket hydrofoil motorboat over my beloved sea to our friends. The cloudless sky was full of peace and beauty. Yet part of my mind was still at the camp, in a world of outcasts, hopeless and broken men, where laws of cruelty and violence rule each desperate day. How different, even behind bars, are those who love God and are filled with His peace.

In the seaport we were welcomed by young people of the Pere-syp church, their sweet faces shining as they heartily congratulated me on my freedom. We went to a believer's home, where we talked and sang and laughed late into the night. I could speak freely, and this made me feel as one risen from the dead! I was bursting with happiness, and I appreciated everything, the warmth of the sun, the beauty and fragrance of flowers, the familiar and dear paths I used to walk along in my youth. I prized this freedom like a price-less treasure, and for a time, it was mine to savor.

Above: Among his family, Joseph is in the first row on the right.

Left: At the Naval Academy in Odessa, 1956.

Below: Joseph (left) with his school friend.

Top Left: Sophomore year in the Naval Academy.
Top Right: Joseph (left) with his brothers.

Preaching at a church service held in a home.

Above: Youth meeting in Kiev, Ukraine, 1965

Below: Local police disrupting a church service.

Left: At a prison labor camp with Yasha (on left) who later became a believer and was baptized in the prison.

Above Left: Engagement photo.
Above Right: Wedding day, September 28, 1969.

Above Left: With Lidia and Vera, 1971.
Above Right: Lidia, Daniel, Vera and Astra the puppy.

Joseph leads a church service in a forest near Riga, Latvia.

One of the many police searches that occurred at Joseph's home.

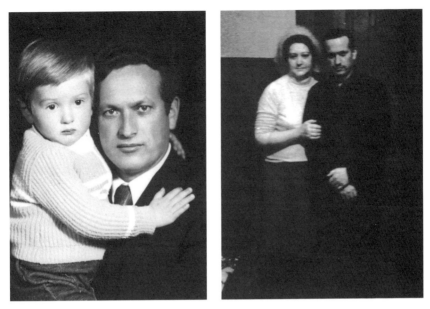

Above left: With son Daniel.
Above right: Maria visiting Joseph in prison in 1980.

Joseph's children anxiously waiting for his arrival after his release
from prison in May of 1981. Kegums, Latvia.

Astronaut Jim Irwin (Apollo 15) sent Joseph a personal note.

Joseph welcomes Astronaut Jim Irwin (Apollo 15) in his church in Riga, Latvia in 1988.

Church of the Cross in Riga, Latvia, which Joseph pastored for 27 years.

Above left: Joseph welcomes Astronaut Charles Duke in Riga, Latvia.

Above Right: Joseph with Luis Palau and Victor Hamm during an evangelistic crusade in Riga, Latvia.

First in history of the Soviet Union an evangelistic crusade in the sport arena of Tallinn, Estonia.

Joseph conducting one of his many outdoors baptisms in Riga, Latvia.

Joseph baptizes new believers in Tobolsk, West Siberia, 1994.

Joseph and Thomas Wang preaching at a maximum security prison in West Siberia.

Above left: Joseph, Charles and Dotty Duke visiting the prison in Krasnodar in which he served his third term.

Above right: Joseph with Richard and Sabina Wurmbrand and Arnold Rose.

Historic moment when the first prayer was held in the KGB Headquarters in Moscow, 1992.

Above left: During the 1992 Billy Graham crusade in Moscow.
Above right: Meeting President Mikhail Gorbachev.

FROM THE SOVIET UNION...

JOSEPH BONDARENKO

Hear:
- The "Billy Graham" of the USSR.
- Why he was in prison for three 3 year terms for preaching.
- How the KGB Colonel who had him imprisoned came to Christ.
- How God is using Joseph today in evangelism in the USSR.

Joseph Bondarenko with Brother Andrew on Red Square in Moscow — March 1990.

With "brother Andrew", President of the Open Doors organization.

Joseph's family performing in Sacramento, California.

Left: Joseph officiating the wedding of his son Daniel and Yana in Santa Barbara, California.

Below: Joseph walking his daughter Mary down the aisle on her wedding day in 2006.

The Bondarenko family. December, 2010.

Joseph with his daughters.

Above left: With his executive assistant and daughter Vera.
Above Right: Fishing with his son and sons-in-law.

Above left: Joseph receives his Doctorate in Theology. May, 2012.

Above right: Joseph and Daniel with the Interim Ukrainian President Turchinov, March 2014.

From left to right: Daniel, Joseph, Vera, Valery Zhakevich, Peter Kravchuk.

Above: The Bondarenko family.
Below: Joseph with his granddaughters, Santa Barbara, CA. Spring, 2014.

Above Left: Joseph with grandson Josef Jr. Summer 2015.

Above Right: My eighth grandchild Amelia Manzuk. January 2016.

Below: Joseph and Maria's family. Summer 2015.

14

My Maria

AFTER BEING RELEASED FROM PRISON, I spent the first three months visiting churches, ministering, and reuniting with friends and family. But one person was on my mind more than any other: Maria.

Since I had mentioned her when I last saw my parents while in prison, she was also on their minds, and they reminded me of her every chance they got. "There is a time for everything, Joseph, and it's time for you to get married," they would say, none too subtly.

I told them how I felt about her, and showed them her picture. Of course, they were smitten, too. "If her soul is as beautiful as her face," my dad said with a grin, "she will be your happiness."

Having prayed countless times about marrying Maria (I even fasted for three days), I felt sure God wanted this union, too. Now all I had to do was ask the woman of my dreams to be mine, forever.

Once I was positive, I was ready to go to her, but I wasn't sure I could catch the train to Brest, immediately as the trains ran on alternate days and it wasn't easy to buy a ticket on short notice. But God took care of the details, and I was able to get that golden ticket. The trip northwest into Belarus would take a full day of travel.

I brought a small suitcase with me filled with luscious "Forest Beauty" pears as a gift for Maria's family. But right before I boarded, the old suitcase fell apart and the pears fell to the ground, rolling everywhere. Was this a sign that she might refuse me? I know, this was a foolish thought, yet I was nervous. After all, she had never declared her feelings for me, although she did send me two postcards and a picture of her. As the fields and forests and groves flew past me on the journey, I hoped for the best. Would she meet me at the station? I fell asleep on the train with thoughts of Maria filling my mind.

It was September 3, 1969, on the morning that train entered the station in Brest, Belarus. The trees were already starting to turn yellow, and there was a cool bite in the air. It wasn't Maria who came towards me on the platform, but Vitaly, her father. My heart sunk, yet I felt encouraged by the broad smile on his face (Maria told me later she felt it would be too forward of her to come and meet me, so she stayed home).

Vitaly Pinkevich and his wife, Anna, were strong believers, and they too had suffered for it. Vitaly, who had used his photography skills as a passport photographer to feed his family during the Great Famine, understood me in a way that few did, as he had been imprisoned for two years for his faith.

Vitaly came to know the Lord during the war, in 1942. He was then a student of Mechanical Gymnasia in Brest, where he attended services under the teaching of the well-known pastor Lukas Dzekutz-Maley. As he soaked in the excellent sermons and observed the pastor's righteous living, Vitaly left his worldly ways and devoted his life to God's ministry.

Maria's mother, Anna Yakovenko, was saved during the war, just like Maria's father. At the beginning of the war, Anna had been sent to West Ukraine as a primary school teacher. She was far from her nearest and dearest. After the front line moved farther on, a missionary from London came to West Ukraine, preaching God's Word. The message touched my future mother-in-law's heart, and she gave her life to Jesus Christ. She was baptized together with her husband in 1942, and soon after that, they got married. Maria was born in 1944, and her mother liked to call her "Musya."

Finally, Vitaly and I got to their home and there she was, the woman I had been longing for. Maria's cheeks were burning. "Why didn't you come sooner?" she asked shyly. "You've been out of prison for three months."

I learned that she had received my two postcards while I was in prison, as I had received her two postcards (a miracle in and of itself, as numerous letters and postcards from my friends and family did not get through the KGB screening). She had been sure I would write her immediately after my discharge in May, yet I had to be certain proposing to her was God's will. So she waited, and at times was filled with anxious thoughts. She began to second-guess herself, and doubt that I truly did have feelings for her. But just when she was on the verge of giving up, Maria received my letter, which didn't have anything romantic in it, yet she felt peaceful: things would work out between us eventually. When she received my telegram, alerting her to my arrival, Maria knew at once I would come with a proposal. And now, here I was, sitting nervously in her parents' home. She was a sight for sore eyes.

Maria was so beautiful, with her long curly hair and her wonderful eyes. That same face that I dreamed of for three years was everything and more as I beheld her.

"I wanted to come so badly," I said, "but this was the soonest I could come. I thought of you every day."

Her parents left for work, and we were alone. Maria offered me some breakfast, but I couldn't eat a bite until the matter at hand was addressed.

"First, we need to answer a very important question," I said, a bit nervously. The moment of truth had come.

We went to the dining room and sat on the sofa. Somehow, I sensed that she knew what I was going to say, and that she was going to give me the answer I hoped for. My anxiety subsided, and I opened my heart to her, sharing my love and asking her to be my wife.

She said yes! I was filled with joy, yet I had to be honest with her and make her aware of what marrying me could entail.

"Anything can happen," I said. "Now is a good time in my life; I have lots of wonderful and trusted friends all over the Soviet Union. But things may change. Friends might betray me. People might report my ministry to the police, and I might even face another prison term at some point—or worse. It's very possible we would not be together all the time."

Without hesitation, Maria answered my fears. "I am ready to follow you wherever the Lord takes us," she said firmly.

Three years of secret prayers for each other were behind us, and everything was clear. She said yes! She wanted me, Joseph Bondarenko, as her husband. I felt like a million rubles, and even better when Maria's parents came back from work and said yes when I asked them for their daughter's hand in marriage.

Our celebration continued when I brought her to Kapitinova to meet my parents, who, like me, were instantly besotted with Maria, the answer to their prayers. Even the dark cloud of the KGB did little to dampen our excitement. While there in my hometown, we were summoned to be interrogated by a KGB major, Fesunenko, who tried to play "good cop" with us.

He "thanked" Maria for "conquering" my heart. "Hopefully," he said, "now Joseph will not be wandering from church to church with his evangelism." Fesunenko was sorely mistaken. Now I had double the strength and energy as before, with Maria by my side. It wasn't the first or last time someone would question Maria's wisdom in marrying me. When we went to the civilian registrar's office to apply for a marriage license, the clerk noticed from my passport that I had been imprisoned twice. "Aren't you afraid to marry this prisoner?" she asked Maria, obviously confused. My love smiled back at her. "No, I'm not afraid," she said, radiant and confident. Maria knew her fate and mine was in God's hands.

The Wedding

We picked our wedding day: September 28, 1969. We were deeply in love and thrilled to be together, yet dark clouds hung in the horizon. Rumors of our wedding date reached the ears of the KGB, who went to work spreading propaganda about us. According to them, we were "dissenters" and our wedding was a cover for what was really going on: a conference of other dissenters and enemies of the state. At one point, I was threatened with going back to prison. Maria and her parents were also summoned to the KGB office and threatened.

My future father-in-law was unshaken by KGB threats, even though they had already made his own life a living terror. "This wedding will happen," he said. "If you arrest Joseph, Maria will be wedded to his portrait (this was possible in those days). We have an absolute right to hold this wedding."

The KGB was disarmed by Vitaly's bold response to them. They were expecting a much more submissive response to their threats.

Wedding preparations were in full swing: invitations were sent all over the Soviet Union and even Czechoslovakia. Near the house on Verbovaya Street, thirty-one wooden tables and benches were set up, as was a sort of podium with an awning over it.

Maria was worried. "What if it rains? What shall we do?"

"The weather will be what we deserve," I answered with a smile.

She kept worrying. God would take care of everything, I assured her. And on the day of our wedding we had a mixture of sun and clouds but not a drop of rain.

Friends poured in from all parts of the Soviet Union, by planes, by trains and by cars. Visitors kept arriving. We received more than fifty congratulation telegrams.

Maria had three maids of honor: her sister Ludmila, Olya Pinkevitch, and Tonya Bondarchuk. On my side I had Misha Arnautov, Peter Peters, and Victor Mosha standing up for me.

There were more than two thousand people at the ceremony, a number far exceeding any we had dreamed of. The guests had to be fed, and Vitaly rose to the occasion, unfazed. He bought much of the food, and relatives and church members from his church helped out a lot as well. The neighbors cheerfully provided lodging for our visitors. Everybody was taken care of, and our joy was full.

Despite all the threats and efforts of the authorities to interfere, our wedding took place.

The KGB, worried that our "dissenter" guests would stage a

demonstration, arranged for extra trains to run between Maria's hometown and places such as Kiev, Lvov, and Moscow so people would go home immediately after the wedding. They were angry they had failed to stop the wedding and warned me I would never enjoy a quiet life of domestic bliss if they had anything to do about it.

Our "honeymoon" was anything but romantic. The KGB dropped in on us day and night, monitoring us constantly. If they saw we were having visitors, we were fined. They refused to give me a residence permit. "We allowed your wedding here in our border town, but we shall not allow you to live here, too."

Another fine example of the Soviet "kitchen" was the registry system. The Soviet government required every citizen to be registered with the local housing administration to have legal residency where you wanted to live (city, town, village, etc.). Anyone could have been denied their registry based on something as flimsy as a missing stamp on one passport—or just because. Even if you tried to obey all the miniscule rules, you could hardly do so since they were constantly changing according to the whim of whichever government official you happened to encounter.

One evening we were informed that militia were coming after us. Vitaly and I grabbed some important documents, and he quickly put on his topcoat before we ran out and escaped through the backyard in the dark of night. Late at night we returned home and found that Vitaly had accidentally thrown on a woman's topcoat—no wonder we hadn't been caught! We all had a good laugh over that.

We dearly wanted to settle in Brest with Maria's family, but it was not to be. Jesus said, "Whenever they persecute you in one city, flee to the next" (Matt. 10:23). And so we were forced to leave Belarus.

Our Adventure

Right before November celebrations (November 7 was in those days the biggest Soviet holiday—the anniversary of the Great October

Revolution of 1917) while still staying in Brest, Maria and I were invited to a large Christian gathering far to the east in Novosibirsk, Siberia, the third biggest city in Russia after Moscow and Saint Petersburg. We checked in for our flight with two small carry-on bags. One bag contained our personal things, and the other one some Christian books for the church in Novosibirsk.

We boarded the airplane and took our seats in the very back. We placed the bag with the books under out seats.

Just moments before takeoff, two men dressed in civilian clothes entered the cabin, walking down the aisle towards us, carefully peering into the passengers' faces. Reaching our row, he stopped and looked closely at me.

"Are you Bondarenko?"

It was a rhetorical question. He whipped out his KGB officer's identity card.

"You are detained. Get off the airplane, now."

He was in such a hurry he didn't ask about our baggage but began walking quickly towards the doorway of the airplane. I realized in that instant he had not noticed Maria beside me. "What about me?" she whispered as I hurriedly gathered my things and got up to follow the officer.

I motioned for her to remain in her seat, and I got off the plane, with the stewardess closing the door behind me. As I walked through the airport with the KGB officer, under arrest, I could hear our plane take off and fly away, with Maria on board.

I had to think. The bag with the Christian books was safely with Maria—or was it? Would she be arrested in Novosibirsk? There was one stopover in Belarus. Would she be safer getting off there instead?

During the flight, a stewardess began to collect information from the passengers about who was getting off where. Maria had a feeling it was unsafe to continue on to Novosibirsk, and decided to get off in Gomel, less than three hundred miles west of Brest.

Clutching both bags, she quickly left the airport in Gomel and caught a bus to the train station. Her goal was to get home and find out what had happened to me. She had cash for a train ticket back to

Brest, but it was very unlikely she could get a ticket that day. People in those days waited day and night for tickets sometimes.

The bags were heavy, but Maria held on tightly to them, afraid to leave them anywhere they might be searched. She begged the young man at the ticket counter for a ticket to Brest, and amazingly, he came through for her. Maria boarded the train for Brest as I was still being interrogated at the KGB office there.

The officials had been ordered to stop me from preaching at the young believers' gathering in Novosibirsk. It was futile for me to try flying anywhere, never mind Siberia, they said. Finally, after several miserable hours at their office and many threats, they let me go home.

Vitaly and Anna were startled and frightened when they saw me arrive in the middle of the night without their daughter.

"Why are you alone? Where is Maria? What happened?"

I told them what had happened on the airplane, and we prayed for Maria's safety. I was sure she would be wise enough to get off the plane in Gomel and return home.

Maria's quick thinking that day resulted in her escaping punishment by the KGB for having those Christian books in her possession. Many people would have lost their heads in such a scary and potentially dangerous situation, but not Maria. It was the first of many tests for her as my wife, and she passed with flying colors.

Together, we faced many trials and periods of fear and suffering, yet from day one Maria was my helper and my joy.

Incidentally, years later, after the Soviet Union opened up, Maria and I were finally able to visit Novosibirsk and minister to the people there. The KGB was wrong, as usual. Maria and I made a great team, and with God's strength and wisdom, there was no stopping us.

15

The Caucasus Mountains

BELARUS DENIED ME RESIDENCY, and I would have faced heavy persecution in my native Ukraine, so Maria and I prayed fervently about where we should go next. God led us to Dzhvardzeni, a remote village in the north of Abkhazia (considered by most governments to be a part of Georgia), situated in the Caucasus Mountains. A hydroelectric power station was being constructed there, and they had lots of work for strong young men.

From the very first day, we understood life would be difficult there. We stayed with a Christian family at first, but soon we were given a small barrack to inhabit at the edge of the village. We had our work cut out for us in our humble little house. Someone had thrown away an old bed frame and a mattress, and we cleaned those up and used them in our humble abode. Maria had brought bedding and curtains, which she put up on the windows. That was about it as far as furnishings, but it was still a palace compared to prison.

Still, it wasn't easy for us to live there, far from friends and family, in a place so remote Maria had to stand for hours in line for some bread, milk, or dried potatoes, only to pay dearly for these staples. Sometimes bear meat was sold at the local market, and we eventually got used to its strange color and texture. A homemade stove heated our house poorly, but it was the only source of heat. We had only cold running water, and even that was only available at certain hours of the day. Soap and detergent were extremely hard to come by, but we did our best to make do.

I was employed as a crane operator, working a hundred-ton lifting crane. The crane was set on top of a mountain and was used to lift massive beams weighing many tons for a steel overpass. It was difficult and dangerous work, to say the least. Yet, when it was raining, my crane operator cabin hung above the clouds and I liked to look beyond the clouds and rejoice at my freedom.

At lunch, I would climb even higher, to the top of the mountain, carpeted with gorgeous wildflowers and plants of all colors. On the mountaintop, I made a small altar of stones and I would pray there daily, remembering my fetid prison cells and praising God for the fresh air, clean, beautiful fragrances, and the babble of the mountain river with its pure water. "I will lift up my eyes to the mountains, from where shall my help come?" (Ps. 121:1).

I picked flowers for Maria and brought them to her every evening.

At my mountain altar, I read my Bible and prayed for Christian brothers and sisters in every region of Russia, people who loved me and had prayed faithfully for me when I was in prison. It was on that mountain that God revealed to me that someday I could preach His message of the Good News about Jesus freely and openly to the people of Russia.

Our young Christian brother Victor used to come pick me up on his motorbike to take me to men's Bible studies in Sukhumi on the coast of the Black Sea, more than ninety miles away northeast over dangerous, bumpy mountain roads. God kept us safe. On Sundays, Maria and I used to visit church services in Sukhumi, traveling by a bus system that was unreliable at best.

I'll never forget the time we almost didn't make it home on a Sunday night. For some reason the last bus destined for our village did not come, and Maria and I were stranded in a town nearly twenty miles from our home. How on earth would we get home? Walking that distance on foot over mountainous terrain in the black night was out of the question. I had work in the morning, and if I failed to show up, forty workers would have to stand idle, and I would be in big trouble with my boss.

The street lamps at the bus stop were all burned out, so we stood there in total darkness. Eventually, a young man approached us and asked how to get to our village. He was going to take a job and it would be his first time there. He made us a party of three.

After a while a Volga drove by slowly and stopped in front of us. There were two men inside, and one of them stuck his head out of the window and said, "Anyone want to go to Dzhvardzeni?" We all jumped in the backseat of the Volga.

The trip was long and bumpy, and at one point the car stopped in the darkness near a large tea plantation. The two men, Georgians, began to argue and shout at each other as we sat there tensely, wondering if the violence would escalate and spill over and involve us.

"Where are you going to take us?" Maria finally ventured, in a trembling voice. "Please, take us home!"

The argument continued for some time, until finally the driver said that he would first take his friend home, and then he would take us to our place. When we returned home, we fell to our knees, thanking the Lord for bringing us home safe and sound.

※ ※ ※

After we had spent six months in our rustic mountain home, Maria's father, Vitaly, came to visit, bringing household items we desperately needed. He was such a wonderful father to both of us, and during his visit he did his best to improve our living conditions. He was surprised to see the primitive conditions in which we lived, with cows at our back door in the morning, mooing for food scraps, and pigs wandering around the village, squealing and burrowing in the ground. Vitaly accompanied me to work a few times and saw how dangerously high the crane cabin hung. When he returned to Belarus, he intensified his search for a new home for his daughter and me.

Moreover, Maria was pregnant with our first child, and in the Caucasus, you had to pay dearly for a maternity home in which to give birth. We decided that Maria would go to Brest, to her parents' home, to deliver the baby.

My mother-in-law, Anna, and Maria's younger sister Raisa were horrified to see our shack-like house and the run-down yard with hungry livestock milling around. They were eager to get themselves and Maria out of there quickly. Before they left, Maria asked me a question. "I assume you want a boy?"

"Why would you say that?" I asked, surprised.

"Many men want their firstborn baby to be a son, an heir."

"No, we need a daughter to help you," I said. "God will decide what we need."

On July 9, 1970, our first daughter was born in Brest. We named her Lidia in honor of Lidia Vins, my friend Georgi's mother and chairwoman of the Council of Prisoners' Relatives. Lidia had gone through great sufferings when she spent three years in prison for her deep faith in the Lord Jesus.

I thanked God beyond all measure for the happy birth of my daughter. But, being in Dzhvardzeni, I was not able to be with them yet. Fortunately, Anna was by her side the whole time. As Maria and Lidia were leaving the maternity home, Anna noticed the staff whispering and exchanging sidelong glances with one another. At the exit, reporters began taking pictures of my wife and daughter.

Why would there be reporters covering the arrival of a poor crane operator's baby? My theory is that they were there because the KGB had been spreading rumors since our wedding that our marriage was in name only, a front for us to hold a believers' conference. After Lidia was born, those rumors stopped cold.

Though I longed to meet my daughter and be reunited with my wife, I was essentially trapped in Dzhvardzeni. The KGB had noticed that in the months we had lived in the mountains, I had been away from the center of church activities and unable to exert much influence. They ordered the local authorities to disallow me to register to leave the vicinity.

But then a wonder took place. A highly unusual snowstorm hit the region, and telephone cables were downed by all the snow. As a result the village officials couldn't clear my departure with their superiors who had the orders from the KGB. I decided to push my luck and attempt to leave.

"Do you have any debts here?" The head of the registration office asked me.

"No," I replied honestly. "I owe nothing to anybody."

Having registered my departure, I made the quickest exit I could out of the village, and traveled to Brest, where I held my firstborn child in my arms for the very first time.

16

Moving to the City of Red Roofs

IN 1969, A TERRIBLE HURRICANE swept over Latvia, and millions of trees were knocked down (Latvia has the fourth highest proportion of land covered by forest in Europe). Newspapers began to announce that workers were needed to clear the woods, and so in 1970, Vitaly and his sons, Peter and Leonid, traveled to Latvia to make some money.

Vitaly wrote to me, telling me he was praying and doing his best to find a suitable place for Maria and me. At the same time, several families in Riga, Latvia's capital city, were praying, asking God to send them a minister. Of course, we knew nothing about this at the time.

In 1971, my father-in-law bought a house in a small village about twenty-five miles outside of Riga. The entire family moved more than three hundred miles north to Latvia, including Maria and me.

Latvia was a huge change for us. Even though it was still in the Soviet Union, it was very different in language, way of life, culture, and its Western style of living. Unlike Ukraine or Belarus, Latvia's citizens often kept to themselves and could be deeply reserved and even cold. Generally it follows that cultures fall into two basic categories, reflecting the relative temperature of their regional climates: some are "hot" and some are "cold." It's much less a personal thing and much more a cultural phenomenon. Within the USSR we experienced both, depending on where we were living.

Still, we warmed quickly to the beautiful city of Riga, the ancient capital of our new country with its more than two million people at the time. Riga was and is the historical, cultural, and economic center of Latvia, and we liked how the buildings and monuments reflected the cultural heritage of the nation. The stunning Dome Cathedral sits near the banks of the Daugava River. Its construction began in 1211 when the Livonian bishop Albert of Riga laid the foundation stone. The Riga Cathedral is known all over the world and is considered the largest medieval church in the Baltic states.

Riga, a pretty and clean city of green parks, lovely fountains, and red roofs, won us over, despite the initial coldness of the people and the dreary, rainy weather.

The year we moved, I was chosen to be a pastor of the independent underground Baptist church in Riga (later, Baptist Church of the Cross that I pastored for 27 years), which met in church members' homes. During the day I was a pastor, ministering and shepherding my flock. But at night, I worked as a laborer at a steam shop, where I fetched countless buckets of coal to feed a large boiler used to provide heat to the large buildings in the area (hospitals, apartments, factories, etc.). Nowadays, pastors are paid by their churches, but I have never been a paid pastor. I had to earn money in other ways to feed my family.

The church grew, and we began to reach out and work shoulder to shoulder with believers in Latvia, Estonia, Finland, and all over the Baltic region, sharing the gospel and opposing atheism. Spiritual renewal was sweeping the land, and friendship and cooperation between God's children became stronger and stronger.

This fervor and unity did not escape the notice of KGB officials. Once again, I received repeated summons to be interrogated about why we had come to Latvia, our intentions, and so on. "Who gave you a residence permit? Who sold a house to you?" They demanded, over and over. "We shall tear your papers to pieces and cancel your registration."

The woman who had sold us our house was also chairwoman of our village council, and she used to come to our house, formerly hers, to break up our services. Years passed, and when I ran into her, she confessed that she had been in big trouble for having sold us the house. I tried to comfort her, telling her God would reward her someday for her good deed.

❈ ❈ ❈

In the summer of 1971 our little Lidia turned one. She was a bundle of energy and joy, and she had her mother's green eyes and curly blonde hair. Her singsong voice rang out all over the house. In September our family expanded, as God gifted us with another sweet baby girl, Vera.

Life, and ministry, went on. We held services in the woods, in apartments, and private houses. Militia and volunteer militia broke up our services whenever they found out about them, fining us all. KGB officers searched sixteen apartments during one nighttime sweep. On another occasion, militia arrived at 6 a.m., flooding windows with flashlights, and shouting, pounding on doors, and demanding to be let in immediately. At our home, they began to break open the locks to our door when we wouldn't open up. My father-in-law, Vitaly, and our relative Raisa held the door shut for as long as they could while we frantically hid Christian books, flyers, and any documents or letters having to do with the Council of Prisoners' Relatives. When the door burst open, the militia found nothing condemning, yet they served me with a subpoena nonetheless. I was ordered to come to the public prosecutor's office in Riga.

On the appointed day, my daughter Lidia became seriously ill and we had to rush her from our small village to a doctor in Riga. When I didn't show up at the public prosecutor's office, KGB officers hurried to my home, where they were met by Anna, my mother-in-law. Anna calmly explained that I had taken my child to a hospital. "Which hospital?" they demanded. She said she didn't know, for there were quite a few hospitals in Riga. Militia men were posted at the train station, waiting for me to come back home.

That evening we stayed in Riga with our friends Mikhail and Klavdia, waiting for Lidia to get well. Vitaly called us there and advised me to not return home, as militia had set a trap for me.

The situation was becoming more dangerous for me by the minute. I met with some trusted friends that night to brainstorm about what could be done. I could be arrested at any time, and if so, would leave the church in a vulnerable position. We decided the best thing for me to do was to go underground, leading the church in secret rather than out in the open.

Illegal

I was now a fugitive, on the run and hiding with believers in Estonia and in other pockets of the Soviet Union. The KGB were combing the country with a fine-toothed comb, looking for me everywhere. My name and photo were on a "most wanted" list, and my home in Latvia was under constant surveillance. I usually had no contact with my family, which was extremely difficult for me—and for them. Maria didn't know where I was or if I was safe or hurt, still free or under arrest somewhere. A local militia officer cancelled my residence registration and said I was forbidden to live in my own home.

I never gathered any moss but kept myself on the run, popping in at church services and even at home when it was possible. Once, I was able to sneak home in the evening, and I asked Maria to prepare food for some brothers who were coming to meet with me at 9 p.m.

At 9 p.m. sharp, there was a knock at the door. I was combing my hair and called for Maria to answer the door. When she went to the door, a spine-tingling instinct stopped her. "Who's there?" she asked.

"It's the militia. Open up." I could hear them from the bathroom. Maria's heart hammered and she prayed that God would protect the new child growing under her heart from her fear.

"Why have you come so late?" she finally said, haltingly. "Couldn't you have come earlier? Children have to go to bed, and you are disturbing them!"

"We will keep pounding on this door until you open up," they said. "We have to find out if anyone criminal is inside your house."

I fled to the secret hiding place Vitaly had made for me in the attic, near the chimney flue. Maria decided to open the door sooner rather than later to avoid making them more suspicious. Indeed, the militia merely checked the rooms of the house and didn't even investigate the attic. Once again, I was safe.

Another time, my brother Peter, who bore a strong resemblance to me, came to the house and helped Maria with some maintenance. Peter was working in a room on the second floor and there were no curtains on the window. Apparently, our neighbors were spying on us and reported that they had seen me.

Suddenly, KGB exploded through the door and demanded to know where I was.

"He's not home," said Maria, startled and confused.

"What do you mean he's not here? He was just seen on the second floor! Shame on you. You call yourself a believer, and yet you are lying!"

She guessed at once they had confused Peter and me. They stormed upstairs without Maria's permission, and their faces lit up when they saw Peter. "See, you're lying! There he is!"

The captain took Peter's passport and barely looked at it, continuing to taunt Maria, calling her a liar and a poor example for a believer.

"Take him down to the station," the captain said, nodding at Peter.

Maria couldn't let that happen. "Look at his passport again and this time, read his name," she said. "This is his brother, who looks like Joseph." They thought they had surely captured me that time, when really they had accomplished nothing more than looking foolish.

❈ ❈ ❈

Maria was about to give birth to our third child, and the KGB were watching her every move, sure that I would materialize and then they could grab me. Where could I hide from their enemy eyes? God answered our prayers again, through the help of a Christian friend, Vasilyev, who invited my pregnant wife to his and his wife's place on the Baltic Sea. Vasilyev's mother, Shura, worked in a maternity home, and she told us to pray that Maria would go into labor during her shift. That way she could then pull strings and get her accepted as a patient.

That's exactly what happened, and on December 29, our son, Daniel, was born. God hid me "in the presence of my enemies" (Ps. 23:5), and I was even able to sneak in to meet my son and bring my brave wife a bouquet of flowers.

Brave and Reliable

The news about terrible persecutions of believers in the Soviet Union was spreading beyond our borders, and believers in other countries were starting to pray for us and look for ways to help prisoners' families in the USSR.

There are endless names and faces in Finland that God sent our way and used to preserve us in those times. Our dearest lifelong friends and laborers in Christ, Hannu and Laura Haukka, were instrumental in raising an awareness in the West of our situation and played an important role helping our family and church survive, both financially and spiritually. They also sent Bibles and other Christian literature into the Soviet Union. The Finns were incredible, praying constantly and even risking their own property and freedom to help us. We saw God working behind the scenes in a powerful and real way.

There was a Finnish acrobat, a believer, who once tried to smuggle Bibles and Christian books across the border to us. The customs agents strip-searched him and confiscated all the literature that had been tied to his body with a thin rope.

Suddenly, the acrobat had an idea and he stood on his head. Even when he was told the search was over and he could get dressed, he continued to ignore them and stood on his head. The customs officers were completely at a loss, and they finally called their boss, who asked the obvious question:

"Why are you standing on your head?"

It was time for him to speak his mind. "I have been to many countries, but in none of them I have been searched like that," he said. "Obviously, in the USSR, everything is upside down. To understand what the Soviet reality is like, one has to stand and walk upside down."

He was set free, but the books remained confiscated, which was no surprise to us. Any book, document, letter, or piece of paper with a Bible verse on it was considered evidence of a crime. Believers were called "spies," and they called the Bible "dynamite." Atheist literature described the Bible as a weapon to destroy the foundation of the Communist state. For once, the enemy was right but didn't have a clue how right they were.

Moving to Riga

A year before we moved from our small village into the city of Riga, Anna was born to our family in February, 1977. Our children were growing and giving us such joy. As I was frequently on the run, it fell upon Maria to be both mom and dad, loving them, disciplining them, and nurturing their tender faith in God.

Lidia was about to graduate from first grade. She was an excellent pupil and an old soul, who loved to recite poems at school and at church. Lidia considered herself to be responsible for her younger brothers and sisters. She taught Vera to read and write before she went to school.

One day at school, the teacher asked the pupils to recite a poem they had learned at home. Lidia was the first to raise her hand. The teacher asked her to go forward and recite her favorite poem. With great expression and an articulation beyond her years, Lidia recited a poem about nature. "OK, Lidia, well done," her teacher said. Lidia waited. "Be seated," the teacher added.

Lidia came home from school in tears. "I recited a poem at literature lesson, and no one said "amen" at the end!" she cried. "Mommy, why did they do that to me?" Our little girl was expecting the whole class to say "amen" in one voice, just as they did at church!

In the spring of 1978, our family moved to Riga, to a small cottage on the edge of the city. The house had been sorely neglected and needed a lot of work, but we figured we had lots of time to fix it up. Lidia was eight, Vera, seven, Daniel, five, and baby Anna was only a year old and just teetering on her first steps.

She would try a few steps and laugh with delight, and when she fell, she cried. But then she would raise her hands to me, her eyes full of trust, knowing I would help and support her as she learned to walk. Can a father ever forget such moments? I cherished my time with my little ones, knowing that perhaps soon I would be ripped away from them.

Before we were even unpacked, we left for Krasnodar on a ministry trip 743 miles south of Moscow, 92 miles northern of the Black Sea port of Novorossiysk via Kharkov. The children stayed home with my sister Nadya. The night before we left, God revealed to me in a dream that I would stay in Krasnodar. I thought this meant I would stay and visit churches, but what ended up happening there was a very different outcome.

17

What Happened in Krasnodar

IN SPITE OF ACUTE EFFORTS by the authorities to hinder the gospel, God was constantly bringing Russian souls to Himself. We were shackled in many ways on the outside but as free as soaring eagles on the inside. Many evangelists were still in prisons, but many others were still free and refused to buckle to KGB pressure and spread the Good News of Jesus Christ whenever they could.

From 1971 to 1977, my life was filled with ministry and evangelism, as I was honored to bring Christ's message to regions in Siberia, Caucasus, Moldova, Ukraine, and Central or Middle Asia, which includes those country names ending with the Persian suffix -*stan*, meaning "land of." At several of the evangelistic meetings I spoke at, hundreds of people gave their lives to the Lord. Still, I faced constant criticism from fellow believers, incredulous that I would take such risks.

Perhaps one of the riskiest ventures of all was the annual youth convention, held May 1–2 in Kharkov, due south of Moscow, and attended by a thousand or so young people from all over Ukraine and other Soviet states.

Leaders from the churches in Kharkov would organize these conventions, scouting good, safe places to hold the meetings, arranging for music and speakers, and inviting believers and unbelievers both.

In the Baltic region, we would try to transport our youth in rented busses without the KGB finding out. We managed to rent an Ikarus shuttle bus for forty people, but by the time we rented it, we had little time to travel hundreds of miles to Kharkov.

We were driving as fast as we could, when suddenly our back tire blew out. It was a holiday, and all the service stations were closed. What could we do? Everyone woke up and prayed. Early that morning, we found a spare tire in a junkyard, but just as we were getting close to Kharkov, two more tires blew out.

I've learned over the course of many years of ministry that when there are great obstacles, great blessings are often on the other side. It was crystal clear the enemy did not want us to get to Kharkov in time for the conference, but we did anyway. When we called some of our friends in the city, they rallied together and brought enough vehicles to pick us all up and bring us to the meetings. Even after three out of four tires malfunctioned on our trip, we were only half an hour late.

The meeting took place in a tent in the large backyard of a believer's house. In the center of a tent there was a sign: "CHRIST IS THE SAVIOR OF THE WORLD," and the number "153" (the number of fish the disciples caught at Jesus' command). The believers fasted and prayed that no less than 153 souls would come to the Lord at the service.

The street was impassible because of the crowd, and soon the yard was packed without a single space for one more person. How could we accommodate all the visitors? I had an idea: We would ask the neighbors if we could pay them for the produce in their gardens in exchange for them allowing us to use their gardens as overflow. Everyone was soon accommodated.

We began with a wedding, which drew some folks curious about what a Baptist wedding looked like. The young couple was wedded, blessed, and everybody congratulated them. Preaching, testimony, and the music of two orchestras followed, and the entire time people came forward to give their lives to Christ.

Having spent a night at friends house in Kharkov, we left by car for Krasnodar, Russia, that is more than three hundred miles southeast of Kharkov (over a thousand miles from home in Riga). The next day, scores of young people came to a prayer meeting at a house on Ryleyev Street in Krasnodar, where they found the gate to the yard to be locked and a watchman standing guard. "The authorities of the city have prohibited the young people's gathering here," he announced.

This and what came after was the KGB's work. We found out later that they had turned the people of the city against us, spreading the word that the Baptist young people were planning a revolt. Right before the event, my picture had been dispatched to all the militia stations of the region, with orders to apprehend me as a dangerous criminal.

Part of me wanted to escape and part of me wanted to be with my fellow believers during this time of crises. The latter part won out as I knew they needed my leadership and support. Maria and I were quite anxious—would I be arrested again and sent to prison? We prayed and felt God directing us to go to our friends Yevgeny and Luba's house. As we approached the house, we came upon Luba pushing a baby carriage with her tiny Olya inside.

My heart stopped. Across the street, there were KGB agents, grabbing believers and shoving them into a bus obviously bound for the militia station. In that moment, I knew I would not escape, and I subtly handed my notebook and camera to Luba, who hid them in the baby carriage.

Almost immediately, I was spotted, and a KGB officer rushed toward me, calling some volunteer militia to back him up. They seized me roughly, twisting my arms behind my back so hard I thought they would snap in two.

"Why are you breaking my arms?" I gasped in pain. "I'm not resisting you!"

"You anti-Soviets must be killed, not just beaten," the captain snapped at me.

When I got on the bus, the young believers started singing a Christian song. The militia captain still didn't realize who I was, and demanded my identification. He couldn't believe it was me.

"We've been looking for Joseph Bondarenko for three days," he said staring at me. "This can't really be you."

He dragged me off the bus, where a militia car took me to the Communist Party district committee office. Accompanied by three officers, I was taken to the private office of a senior secretary of the district committee. Their faces were gleaming with pride. They had nabbed the ringleader of the citywide Baptist "revolt"!

The secretary, Medunov, a corpulent man who barely fit in his huge, luxurious armchair, smiled at me mockingly.

"Don't you know how powerful Soviets are? During the war I used to shoot fools like you by the dozens, just for fun. We shall make your conditions here such that you remember this place all your life—if you live. Here, you will forget your very name."

He spit and swore.

"My God is stronger than you and He will protect me," I said. My arms were throbbing and my heart was pounding. I stared at him right in the eye until he became uncomfortable.

"Put cuffs on him and take him out of my sight," he ordered.

I was detained and taken to Chapayevskoye militia station in Krasnodar. My right arm was dislocated, and the handcuffs cut into my flesh painfully. I was thrust into a cell so humid and hot, the asphalt floor melted the soles of my shoes. My preaching suit hung heavily on my body as sweat dripped off my face.

I could hear the voices of my young brothers and sisters who had been arrested out in the yard. My dearest Christian siblings were there with me! Then I heard the loud voices of militia officers. "Send them away—some to a railway station, and some to the airport." They were being released, and though I was glad for them, I knew in my heart I would remain in custody for a long, long time.

18

Under Scrutiny

AFTER FIFTEEN DAYS, PER STATE Persecutor's decision I was transported to Krasnodar prison. I once again heard the bitter clank of metallic doors, so familiar to me. I was once again in isolation, and the world became so small. When would I see my dear wife, my children, and my parents again? Only God knew.

The following day I was called to meet with the senior investigator of the city office of the public prosecutor. I remembered his last name, Negoda, which means "bad" or "unfit," and I must say it did not suit his character. He turned out to be more honest and just than all the others who had pleaded my cases before. "Honestly, I am not familiar with believers and their teachings, but I will do my best to examine everything thoroughly. I don't understand why you are here, and I will do my best to have you discharged," he said.

"Thanks for your efforts," I said sincerely. "But they all are useless."

A week passed. He called me in to his office again. This time the determination on his face was gone, replaced by defeat.

"The investigators here in Krasnodar agreed to discharge you, but both the KGB and the officials in Moscow want you to get a three- to four-year prison term," he said, sighing. "You're right—there's almost nothing I can do for you."

I appreciated his genuine desire to help me, and his interest in the things of God. Negoda would come to my cell and visit, not always strictly for work. He wanted to learn more about Christianity and my way of living.

I agreed to have a lawyer represent me this time so I could keep in touch with my family through him. Peter, an older man and a war veteran, was assigned to my case and instantly I could tell he was a decent man. During our meetings, we couldn't speak but instead communicated in writing, as the place was wiretapped.

I also tried to witness to him on paper, but he was resistant.

"Joseph, what God are you talking about? You should deny God, and enjoy your freedom. Take everything you can get out of life. You can live very well without God."

Peter did not live long enough to represent me in court. Tragically, he died suddenly of a heart attack.

❈ ❈ ❈

At the pretrial hearing, I was once again confronted with "eyewitnesses" whom I was seeing for the first time in my life. I had the chance to ask one of these witnesses, a student, how much he had been paid to take the stand against me.

"Sixty rubles," he said, unapologetically. "I have to earn a living somehow."

Other paid witnesses, carefully tutored by the KGB, lied openly as they avoided eye contact with me. I thought of Jesus, who had been condemned unfairly and slandered by false witnesses, yet he fervently prayed for them. "Father, forgive them!"

After the pretrial hearing, I was moved to a cell with five men. One of them was a KGB plant, I could tell by the look in his eye when he met me. His job was to pump me for incriminating information.

Later, I found out this "prisoner" was a full-fledged agent. He was quiet but stealthy, always working his angle and trying to start debates in the cell about politics. The agent tried many times to "subtly" get out of me the location of an underground printing office.

It was no use, of course, but still, his crafty pestering wore on me, like the little biting bugs that crawled out of the wall, and the lice that scuttled on my head.

After three months with no success, my cellmate was "put on probation." I immediately began to feel better the minute he left. Now all I had to deal with were fleas and lice.

Another of my cellmates was notable, because he had been an ex-assessor. He used to be the guy who was instrumental in helping to convict criminals, and everyone hated him for it. This man was in a state of constant anxiety, and would walk around the cell, back and forth, like a pendulum. A hardened thief in our cell used to taunt him and flick him on his forehead so many times he developed a knob.

I tried to convince them to leave the poor fellow alone, but they were unrepentant: he had turned the likes of us in many times, and now he had to pay. In prison, returning evil for evil was par for the course.

Every evening, some of the prisoners would throw bread crumbs out of the cell window, and the sparrows and other birds would rush towards the treats in a great frenzy of joy and singing. Their exuberant twittering lifted our spirits, and we looked forward to that bright spot in our dull days. But when the guards picked up on the fact that we were experiencing even a moment of happiness, they tried to stop it.

"It's not a resort around here," they railed at us. "Don't forget you are behind bars!" As if we could forget. Sometimes we would get into trouble for feeding the birds, and we would be denied our daily walk or a visit to the library. Mostly, it was just something for them to try and squash, and they issued empty threats. We loved to lure the birds to us with the bread crumbs. For us, as slaves in shackles, it was precious communication with creatures that were wonderfully free.

One day, a woman who was passing out newspapers for prisoners handed to me a note from my wife. Next door to this woman lived a Christian sister, and she persuaded her to pass me the note. The woman was hesitant; she knew my cell was under special surveillance. But eventually she agreed. From the note, I learned about Apollo 15 astronaut James Irwin's arrival in Moscow and in Riga. Now this was something to smile about.

Before my arrest, my Finnish friend Hannu Haukka (the President and CEO of GCM Ministries, Great Commission Media Ministries [formerly IRR/TV]) had told me about Irwin, a believer and American astronaut. He served as Lunar Module pilot for Apollo 15, the fourth human lunar landing; in 1971 he was only the eighth human to walk on the moon. After retiring from the US Air Force, he traveled the world and served, in his words, as a "Goodwill Ambassador for the Prince of Peace."

So I had made up my mind at that time to invite him to our church in Riga, even though some of my brothers in the church council thought I was crazy. Why would a famous American astronaut come to our church in Latvia? But I thought it was worth a shot, and felt God had given me the idea, crazy though it may be.

I had invited Irwin to Riga, believing he would come, but not knowing he would come while I was in prison.

I was overjoyed! How long had I been waiting for that moment! Yes, it was disappointing that I could not even meet him, never mind arrange all the evangelistic meetings I had been planning.

But he was coming—that was the main thing. Irwin's visit was crucial in many ways. At that time, antireligious propaganda sold the idea that only uneducated, unimpressive people believed in God. James Irwin was a highly educated and extremely accomplished man who also happened to have strong faith in Jesus. I wanted my countrymen to know that Christ was for everyone, including a man who had walked on the moon.

Irwin's story inspired me deeply. While he walked on the moon, he recited Psalm 121. "I knew my help came from the Lord. He made the moon and He was the one who gave me the opportunity to leave my footsteps on its surface," he once said.

Even though I didn't meet him at that time, James Irwin was already a friend to me. When he landed in Moscow in 1978, I was then under examination in Krasnodar. He attended a reception in Moscow, and at this event gave the chairman of the Council of Ministers of the USSR, Kosygin, a petition to release me. "I am here in the Soviet Union on the invitation of Joseph Bondarenko," he said.

"He is a criminal and, consequently, he is in prison now," Kosygin replied, startled.

Irwin was firm. "No, he is not a criminal," he said. "I know that for sure. He is my Christian brother and I am interceding for him and asking your permission to see him personally. That's why I have come here. Where is your freedom for believers, the freedom written about in Soviet newspapers?"

We were not allowed to meet, but, on his petition, I was allowed to have a Bible and a five-minute meeting with my wife. I was grateful to my Christian brother who had never met me yet had stood up for me so bravely.

Maria and the children came to the prison for our meeting, a short visit in the presence of the chief warden. We were all heartbroken when they wouldn't allow the children to come into the meeting. I could hear them crying their eyes out in the hallway, and my heart was wrenched.

They were true to their word: Maria and I had five minutes together and then it was over. She left me with the greatest gift of all: God's Word. I was ecstatic to once more hold the Book in my hands, and I stayed up all night, hungrily reading verse after life-giving verse.

My cellmates were very curious about this book, the contents of which sent me to prison three times! Everybody wanted to touch it and rifle through the holy pages.

My cherished Bible sparked no end of debates and discussions, and I was thrilled to be able to back up my arguments, chapter and verse.

One cellmate asked me lots of questions about the Old Testament, as he was a Jew. A friendship developed between him and me, and I encouraged him as he dealt with depression and deep disappointment over how his life had turned out. Condemned to ten years in prison, he was awakening to the devastating fact that his friends in high places were not going to help his cause as they had promised. All his wealth and status had been taken from him quickly and finally. He had nothing to live for.

We would pray together often, which seemed to lift his spirits.

He was soon moved to a different cell. A few days later, we heard the sounds of a terrible fight going on in the hallway. My Jewish friend had instigated a fight to try and get back in our cell. After three days in isolation as punishment, he got his wish and returned. He was a sorry sight, with his black-and-blue face, his split lip and crooked nose. But he was happy.

"I got my way and I'm back with you," he said, with a lightness that belied his broken face. "Now, read to me from your Book."

Alas, the authorities were on high alert concerning me, and soon after Irwin's return to the United States, my Bible was confiscated. After all, to them it still and always would be a dangerous weapon.

19

The Third Verdict

ON AUGUST 1, I WAS transported to the court for the first day of my trial held in Krasnodar. But that's not at all that happened.

Maria remembers seeing me get out of the *voronok* in the parking lot of the courthouse that day. She knew immediately something was drastically wrong. I don't remember anything from that day, but I got out of the car very slowly, almost like I could barely walk. Maria said I looked more dead than alive. She was terrified but couldn't get anywhere near me.

Apparently, we made eye contact as I was sitting on a bench waiting to enter the courtroom. Maria was sure I was deathly ill, and it was all she could do to keep her emotions in check. She was one of the first witnesses called, and I stayed in the hallway during her testimony.

At some point between then and when I was to enter the courtroom, I had a heart attack, apparently passing out right there in the hallway. Maria saw an ambulance pull up to the courthouse and she knew it was for me.

I was in and out of consciousness, but I did overhear some-one instruct the doctor in the ambulance to misdiagnose me so I wouldn't receive the proper treatment. I also heard the doctor dis-agree. "I took a Hippocratic oath, and I am not going to break my word." The trial was postponed indefinitely.

Maria and my family knew nothing about my well-being, though they went to the prosecutor's office every day to see if they would tell them anything about my condition.

"As soon as he recovers, the trial will resume" was all the details they received. She didn't know if I was on death's door or how seri-ously ill I was, and she ached to be with me. It was especially cruel of the authorities to keep Maria in the dark about my health. She longed to be with me and to lend me her strength and comfort, and I longed to have her by my side. But it was not to be. Three days later, they decided to resume the trial, even though I was weaker than a kitten and barely able to sit, let alone stand. I was escorted into the hall by an officer, and I saw Maria, my mother-in-law, Anna, my brother Vasily and his wife Tamara, my sister Nadya and my nephew Pavel, and my dear children. I couldn't get close to them, but I could hear my five-year-old Daniel crying and begging to see his daddy.

According to prison rumors, I had the harshest and most ruth-less judge of all presiding over my case. With Judge Korolikhin be-hind the bench, I could expect the most severe penalty possible.

"Stand up. The judge is here," the bailiff called out. Oh, how I hated those words. My name was read, and then my birth date and year and the charges against me.

Korolikhin read the indictment, which included the following:

"J. Bondarenko, one of the authoritative Baptist leaders, op-poses existing laws about religious cults. Living in Riga, Latvia, he systematically organized and held mass gatherings of young peo-ple . . . On May 8, 1978, a crowd of about four hundred people, mem-bers of an unregistered Baptist sect, gathered on Ryleyev Street in Krasnodar, near a house of prayer. The crowd of Baptists filled up the sidewalks as well as a part of the road, impeding walking and driving. In loud voices, they sang religious songs, shattering the peace and quiet of the neighborhood . . ."

The judge listed the witnesses, including a commissioner of religious affairs in Latvia, who had lied outright with his statement. My heart sank when the judge also read the names of some of the church members from Krasnodar. Silently I prayed, *May God forgive their weakness and their fear of those who hold power only in this world.*

The hearings continued for two days. Many of the witnesses were paid off, as usual. Particularly strange was the testimony of a big, muscular militia lieutenant colonel, who accused me of stepping on his foot and tearing off the sole of his boot! Of course, this never happened.

In the end, the public prosecutor asked that I be sentenced to three years of imprisonment in a high-security prison.

I was given an opportunity to say final words in my defense:

"Comrades, judges: When you accuse us as believers with causing disorder and chaos, you know it's nothing more than a farce.

"To be rejected by the world and to be judged unjustly for believing in God is a great honor. The Bible says, 'Blessed are those who have been persecuted for the sake of righteousness, for theirs is the kingdom of heaven.'

"I taught our young people to be honest, diligent, righteous, and to respect their elders. My conscience is clear, and I can look people in the eyes with no shame whatsoever. I have committed no crime.

"With God's help, I will again travel the path of suffering. I will take my love for God and my faith in Him to the basement cells of your prisons, and I will also carry with me your names, the names of my persecutors. I will be praying for all of you constantly. God is powerful to forgive your lawless actions, but these deeds can never be undone.

"I know in three years I will be 'rehabilitated' and set free, but the question is, will you be rehabilitated and set free by God? Today you have a chance to set things right, to act justly. I am not a criminal, and you know that."

There was a hush in the courtroom, and Judge Korolokhin cleared his throat before reading the sentence: "The defendant J. Bondarenko is guilty of the charges brought before him, and according to the Criminal Code of the Russian Soviet Federation Socialist Republic, he is sentenced to a penalty of three years of imprisonment in a high-security prison."

My third high-security prison term commenced that day in another cold, dark cell, indistinguishable from the others. My cries of despair had turned to howls, because now I knew all too well what I was facing. And now, I was facing it being apart from Maria and my children. *Oh Lord, how will I survive this cup set before me?*

❄❄❄

There's an interesting PS to this part of my story. Before flying back to Riga, Maria felt nudged by God to go to the judge, Korolikhin, who had lived up to his harsh reputation and had shown me no mercy. She wanted to ask him to return our family photo albums, which had been confiscated as evidence in my trial and brought to the public prosecutor's office in Krasnodar.

When she entered his office, he didn't seem at all surprised to see her. Maria introduced herself, although he knew who she was, and explained the purpose of her visit.

"There's a parable in the Bible about a persistent widow who comes to plead her case with a judge, over and over again," she told Korolikhin. "I'm not a widow, technically, but I am begging you in God's name to please return those family photos."

She also quoted a line from the Russian poet Lermontov, "God's judgment is inevitable." Korolikhin was quiet for a moment, and finally he spoke with a humility that must have cost him dearly. "Can also my sins be forgiven?"

"Yes, of course," Maria replied. "You just have to repent, and you will be forgiven." My wife and the judge talked for some time, as she tried to convince him to give his life to the Lord. All at once, his moment of humility had passed, and he refused to repent, or to give her back the photo album.

Maria finally left his office, feeling it was useless to stay any longer. "I'll pray for you and your family," she said softly, fighting back tears. She was bitterly disappointed about the outcome of her visit. But just a couple of minutes later, as she was still making her way down the flights of stairs, crying and angry, she heard Korolikhin's voice. "Mrs. Bondarenko, come back!" She climbed the stairs again, and at the top, she saw Korolikhin, holding out two photo albums for her. Something touched the heart of that hardened, miserable man that day. Until heaven, we won't know just how deeply.

20

A Third Prison Term

A WEEK AFTER THE TRIAL, I was taken in a *voronok* from my prison to Yelizavetinskaya, a northern suburb of Krasnodar, to a high-security labor camp. My heart was so heavy. To face three years away from my loved ones seemed almost unbearable. Even when I was "free," I rarely saw my family after I went underground with my ministry. Now I wouldn't see them for years, and they would grow and change without me. My heart was broken.

When I got to the prison, I used the one thing that hadn't been stolen from me: I prayed. *Lord, You know my way, I am in Your hands.* In my short prayer, I poured out all the pain of my suffering heart. I asked Him to give me strength for the years of separation.

From my previous prison experience, I knew it was better to declare myself a believer immediately. This preempted any crazy rumors (such as child sacrifice) that might be spread by prisoners with too much time on their hands.

In that prison, I was reunited with a Christian friend, Vitaly, who had been director of a church choir in an Evangelical Baptist

Church. He was just fifteen days away from ending his five-year prison term. Of course, he too had been locked away for his faith in God.

What a joy to meet my Christian brother! In prison, it was rare to have time with a brother, and now there were the two of us. For fifteen days we were His church, as Jesus said, "Where two or three have gathered together in My name, I am there in their midst" (Matt. 18:20).

We shared everything—our sorrows and our joys. We talked about the church, our families, and shared the Lord's Supper together, praying together and building each other up. The fifteen days passed quickly, and Vitaly was set free. I watched out the cell window as he bounded towards his wife and children. I observed as the happy family embraced one another, and soon they walked to the bus stop, and out of my sight.

※ ※ ※

Day by day, my life as a prisoner went on. I was put to work as a metal lathe operator, although I had no experience working with a lathe. On the third day, I was given an impossible schedule of output, and punished if I couldn't produce the required quota.

It was freezing in the lathe shop, and the smoke in the air made my eyes sting. The lathes were old and rusty, and they would break down constantly. Red hot shavings would fly everywhere, causing burns on any piece of exposed skin. We were not allowed to walk away from our machine, even to avoid a fiery shaving. That was considered a violation.

There was a brickyard opposite the camp. Young believers used to slip through the brickyard to try and talk to me through the fence. Two Christian friends, Valery Zhakevich and Peter Kornienko, came to visit me several times. One day, an armed guard happened by and began to chase them. I was awake all night, wondering if they had escaped or not. Much to my relief, the next morning everything was quiet at camp and I had not been called in to the prison office. This meant Peter and Valery had not been detained. Those two continued to visit me many times, despite great risk to their own personal freedom. I can't express how much those visits boosted my spirits.

How lonely and depressed I would have been without those visits, and also the letters sent to me by believers! Each one was a lifeline. It's remarkable that I was allowed to receive them.

One day the prison fire chief called me to his office and gave me a jar of honey and a piece of lard. "It's from your church friends," he said. "I couldn't refuse such good people." I was astonished. How wonderful that food tasted, like manna from heaven! The fire chief and I had many wonderful conversations, and he used to listen attentively to my testimony. Another seed was planted, and another hopeful result to wait for in heaven.

Of course, the KGB soon heard rumblings of these good things, and they demanded I be moved to another prison camp, not knowing that anywhere I went, the God of all good things followed me. Try as they might, they couldn't legislate the way God moved in people's hearts. Despite the actual cold conditions, by tossing me around in a game of spiritual "hot potato" my captors were actually helping certain prisoners come to know the Lord, though I must admit that I still deeply desired to get out and stay out of their hands.

Maria's Trials

Of course, I wasn't the only one who desired my release. Maria was thirty-five when I went to prison for the third time. She was a young woman left alone with the tremendous responsibility of raising four children: Lidia (nine), Vera (eight), Daniel (six), and Anna (fourteen months). Because I had been arrested and jailed, the KGB continued their surveillance of Maria, which made her life difficult and dangerous. She required a tremendous amount of wisdom to protect her children, explain to them why their dad was being kept in prison, and help them realize the dangers surrounding our family.

The children had to watch every word, for if they misspoke, it could lead to more troubles for me and Maria.

The most heartbreaking night for her was when she had to return home to her children with news of their father's arrest. It was certainly traumatic for them to absorb such a horrible update, news they were not able to comprehend. Maria was bombarded with questions that night, and she prayed desperately for wisdom, to know what to say and what not to say. She comforted Lidia and Vera as they cried through the night.

The emotional and physical anguish took its toll on Maria. Shortly after my arrest, she became very ill with a thyroid deficiency, which weakened her and caused her to lose substantial weight. Yet, there was no time for Maria to think of herself, as every child needed her special attention in dealing with their own experience of the trauma caused by the separation of imprisonment. Their dad was gone, and he had been declared an enemy of the Soviet people. There were consequences for them to pay in school and in the community. Maria told me later she had to pretend that all was normal and fine, yet it was far from the truth. As she parented by herself, under grueling circumstances, she clung to the Lord, who carried her every step of the way.

Maria was terribly afraid sometimes that the hardships, persecution, mistreatment, and uncertainty would turn the hearts of her child away from a loving God. What if they decided to go astray, simply because it was too much to handle, too much to understand, and too much to ask of them? We both knew of many children raised by Russia's most courageous warriors for God who nonetheless had turned away from Christ and chose the world instead. Some of these children had become orphans when their fathers were executed for the sake of the gospel. Maria diligently prayed and expressed her concern to the Father, and entrusted the fate of her children into His caring hands.

To add to her troubles, Maria was in constant danger of being betrayed by neighbors, friends, and even church people. The KGB had a whole system of going into people's workplaces and brainwashing them. Many believers were also called to governing offices to be "informed" of the danger of my ministry, or even presented with falsified statements about my arrest.

Believers in our local church were threatened and discouraged from helping our family financially (Maria was a homemaker and didn't have any income after I was arrested). Even just visiting or having any contact at all with her was disadvised. Some of our relatives were afraid to visit us or approach our house. She had to be on guard 24/7 and always aware of her whereabouts. Every day was a challenge and an opportunity to see God at work. She learned to lean on Him deeper than before and run to Him for everything.

Maria's plight was multifaceted and daunting. As a young woman she also had to face considerable temptation from other men, who preyed on her loneliness and the fact that she was without a husband for what would be three years. One of the younger men had tried his utmost to get Maria to be with him. "Maria, do you really intend on waiting for three years until Joseph gets home?" he mocked her. "Don't be ridiculous!" Maria overcome these temptations with the power of the Holy Spirit, and surrendered her desires to the Lord. These temptations occurred many times in those days. Maria couldn't find strength in herself but relied on God's strength to gain victory and keep her wedding vows until my return.

A Family Reunion

After spending almost a year in Yelizavetinskaya labor camp, I was transferred to a prison in urban settlement Tlyustenhabl, Adygea Republic, about twenty one miles east of Yelizavetinskaya. After five months in the new prison, in Tlyustenhabl, I learned I was to have a visit from my wife and children.

I could hardly wait. How I loved them all from my prison cell! I knew every step of my long-suffering way was accompanied with their prayers.

First, I counted the time in months, then weeks, days, and finally minutes. And then there she was, in my arms again, my dearest love, Maria.

My daughter Vera remembers this visit vividly:

> Our visit to prison to see Dad made a great impression on us children. I was nine years old. We prepared for the trip with anticipation, trying to be good for Mama, and helping her pack nice things for Dad to eat, like candy, coffee, tea, sausages, lard, and the dried fish Dad liked so much. In those years, there was often a shortage of food, so whenever anyone treated us to chocolates or sweets, we saved them for our visit with Dad. He wasn't allowed to receive a package from us, but we were allowed to eat meals together with him during our visit. Mum brought some meat to make a tasty soup for this very special meal.
>
> We couldn't wait to see Dad, and each day we tore off sheets of a loose-leaf calendar, believing somehow it would make the time go faster. We weren't just excited about seeing our father but also about flying in an airplane for the first time. The trip was a huge adventure for us. Daniel was five, and he sat anxiously on Mum's lap the whole trip, repeatedly asking her if we were going to "fall down."
>
> When our flight from Riga arrived in Krasnodar, we learned that everyone had been very nervous about our flight, as one of the engines had been not working properly.
>
> "Uncle Sergei," a Christian friend of a certain age (and therefore an honorary "uncle"), met us at the airport and took us to the prison camp in Tlyustenhabl. It took forever for us to get through the checkpoint at the prison; they went over every last item we brought with a fine-toothed comb. The officials confiscated the coffee and chocolate at once. Finally, accompanied by an officer on duty, we made our way through an endless hallway, with many doors. Dad was behind all those doors—we could hardly believe it.
>
> We were shown into the room where we would meet Dad. At the end of the hallway was an old, dirty kitchen with a do-it-yourself oven made by prisoners.
>
> We spent a few hours waiting for dad to get out of work.

Meanwhile, Mom was setting the table, so that everything would be ready before he came. I stood at the barred window that was smeared with paint, trying to spot Dad in a group of prisoners returning from work. My heart constricted as I saw those skinny, gray, and exhausted faces. Our beloved Daddy was among those! There are no words to describe the pain and confusion in my child's heart.

Finally, the warden on duty brought Dad to us, and we threw our arms around his neck. It was so strange to see him looking like that, in black prison clothes, with a buzz cut, his skin the ashen gray color common to all the prisoners.

Why such injustice? He was neither a criminal nor a thief, but he was given place amongst those! Our hearts were exploding with bitterness and resentment. Why did we have to meet him there, in prison, while children our age could freely spend time with their fathers in museums, exhibitions, or out in nature? But yet this experience drew us closer as a family, and we all became mature fast as we saw these bleak realities firsthand.

My baby sister Anna was only two years old. She called Dad "Uncle" and the first day was afraid to approach him. By the evening, she warmed up to him, and by the last two days he pretended he was a horse and the two of them "galloped" along the hallways with her shrieking delightedly on his shoulders. Within those gray prison walls, we could somehow let loose and be kids, running and playing with our beloved father.

Yet, we were acutely aware of being watched and listened to by the authorities. From the time we were small, we were all trained by our parents to be extremely careful in what we said out loud. We knew the KGB had bugged the room, and when Mum told Dad the church news she wrote it on a piece of paper for him to read and then tore it up into tiny pieces.

On that visit, Lidia told Dad something that had happened while he was gone. Mum had left us alone at home one day while she went to prayer meeting, and we decided to play "church" and pretend we were having a service. Lidia was enthusiastically reciting a poem when suddenly she had stopped.

"Quiet!" she whispered urgently. "Dad's here! I just heard him call my name!"

We were thrilled and ran towards the door to greet him. But nobody was there. Then she heard his voice again. "Lidia. Lidia!" Again she looked through the peephole, expecting to see Dad, but there was no one there. "Lidia." She heard her name again, and this time she knew for certain. "That's Dad, for sure!"

She ran outside in the yard. We all followed her, and at the very end of the street we saw a man walking, and soon he passed out of our sight. We came back into the house, but Lidia would not calm down: "That was *Dad's* voice—I know that for sure." We got on our knees and prayed fervently for our father. We knew somehow he needed us to pray for him right then and there.

When we told him this story, Dad began to think about what was happening to him during that time period. He eventually realized that the very day Lidia heard his voice was the day the KGB had sent a hardened killer to stab him to death. He had been in mortal danger that day, and God had kept him safe with the prayers of his children covering him.

Every night of our visit we talked late into the night. We slept as a family in a prison barrack. One night Lidia and I heard some rustling under our beds. Rats were gnawing at the potatoes we had brought for Dad. Lidia and I did not sleep a wink the whole night.

We dreaded leaving Dad all alone in that terrible place again, but on the third day we had to pack up our things. By noon we had to vacate the "reunion room."

With tears streaming, we all clung to Dad until we heard the guard's voice, telling us the visit was over. Dad committed us all into God the Father's hands, and blessed each one of us. Turning away from us, the guard escorted our father back to prison.

✄ ✄ ✄

A year before my discharge, I was moved to a prison work site as a crane operator. The work in the entire camp had stopped when the previous crane operator had been released. For a long time, prison officials were hesitant to trust me with the job without the approval of the KGB.

But, since I was the only one who could actually operate a crane, they had no choice.

My friends Mikhail, Yevgeny, Alexander, and Sergei used to approach the camp and wave up at me as I sat high atop the prison camp in my crane cabin. I was thrilled to see my Christian brothers, and "meet" with them in such a way. Often, they would point to the sky, and I knew what they were trying to say. *In heaven there is the One who knows everything, sees us, and thinks of us. Don't give up, Joseph!*

Connecting Links

Letters from the outside world were a lifeline, a window to freedom. I received about two letters per day, and on Christmas and Easter, I could receive as many as eighty precious letters. Each missive passed through three censors: the prison censor, the criminal investigation department, and the KGB. Talk about modern-day miracles!

Each letter from home was like a mini-holiday for me. How much love and warmth I could feel in every line! Maria's letters were most cherished, her words being loving and profound. Once she even tucked a napkin doused with her perfume in a letter, and somehow the censors let me have it. Her scent, along with her words, made her feel not so far away.

Our letters were a thread between our hearts. We were inspired by the faith we shared, our spiritual unity, and our understanding of each other. The Lord gave us strength to stay faithful to our wedding vows and to live in hope.

Prison censors took Maria's letters home to read them to their wives. They used to marvel about her to me. "You have an amazing wife, Joseph," they said. "She is your happiness."

They were more right than they knew. Maria's sacrificing love, devotion, and care for me and our children gave me strength to endure those hard days. I understood in a deeper way that my wife was a crown, my consolation, and the treasure of my heart.

Many were the days I returned to camp from work, bone-tired, shuffling my feet, but when I entered the barrack and saw her letters piled on my bed, the stress would melt away in a second.

I would read her words, and I'd be there, among my friends, at home, in my church. "Like cold water to a weary soul, so is good news from a distant land," wrote Solomon in Proverbs 25:25. He was correct. In every sentence I read between lines, trying to grasp what had not been said. I kept the letters carefully, and would re-read them over and over.

I was allowed to write my close relatives only twice a month, and the rule was that we could not write about ourselves or the difficulties of prison life. Thus, Maria and I came up with a code, some prearranged expressions and words, so I could learn news of family and church, and she could get a sense of what was going on with me.

If Maria wrote that someone's children "went on an excursion," it was a message that someone had been arrested. "A good harvest of apples and pears" meant new souls had come to know the Lord. And if she wrote that the children were sick, that meant there had been searches, surveillances, and interrogations.

I also treasured my children's letters, their childlike handwriting, their thoughts and wishes filled with genuine love and concern. "Dad, you have stayed there too long! Come home soon!" "Uncle Chief [the prison warden]: Let Dad go. He loves us very much and he has done no harm to anybody." I used to fall asleep holding their letters, hearing their sweet voices and feeling their prayers.

My little ones also endured persecution, in the form of humiliation and jabs from their classmates and teachers because their father was behind bars. Teachers would dock their grades for no reason, and Lidia and Vera were expelled from their music school in their second year even though they were doing well.

Vera wrote me to tell me this sad news. She complained about such injustice, as she was aware why she and her sister were truly expelled. They were innocent children, unable to comprehend the crafty intentions and treacherous principles of the atheist state. The authorities did their best to show our kids that there was no place in educated Communist society for believers. Having believing parents was just the first strike against them. From the time they were small, my children knew all too well that faith could mean suffering.

Any time my children suffered, it tore me to pieces. *Lord, give us all strength to endure these abuses and help me to pray for and bless those who hate us.*

Back Home

The spring of 1981 was very special to me. My third prison term was finally over—I could hardly believe it.

Before my discharge, I was sent for by a chief warden, who was joined by a KGB officer. "If a large group of believers come here tomorrow and hold a demonstration, you will be taken at once to another prison in Rostov by helicopter," the warden said. "So, it's your choice if you will be discharged from here tomorrow or discharged from Rostov, who knows when."

I didn't know anything about any demonstrations, I told him honestly, but I knew my relatives were going to come to welcome me out of prison.

On May 8, 1981, after an hours-long search of my person and my meager possessions, including the letters, I was released. The prison officials read through every letter and every note I took, and returned only the letters (as they had already checked them three times!).

They took civilian clothes from Maria and gave them to me so I could get changed. I was given a certificate of release—"a prisoner's passport," and, accompanied by a dozen officers, I was taken out of the prison to freedom.

As I was leaving, the boss of my work site called out to me. "Joseph, when you have time, come to us. Don't forget us!"

Again, the sun seemed to shine more tenderly as I breathed in my first gulps of free air. My wife ran up to me and gave me a huge bundle of tulips. My relatives who had arrived from Riga hugged me and thanked God. We drove a bit farther from the camp, and there on the side of the road stood believers young and old from the church in Krasnodar. They, too, were overjoyed at my release, and I was touched by their show of solidarity. *Thank you, God—once again I am a free man!*

❊ ❊ ❊

Come to us when you have time . . . I could hear the prison boss's words in my mind for a long time. I didn't know how or when, but I resolved to go back to the prison in Tlyustenhabl near Krasnodar and preach the Good News to those prisoners desperate to hear it.

But ten years would pass before I could fulfill my promise to the prison boss.

21

A Homecoming

A WEEK AFTER MY RELEASE from prison, we finally made it home to Latvia, and the countryside was showcasing an especially verdant spring season that year. It was a perfect, cloudless day, and the flowering trees were blossoming in a profusion of color and fragrance.

There were flowers everywhere, especially at my house, because they were grown there with love and tender care by Vitaly, my father-in-law who had become a second father to me. He was a master tulip grower, and in fact grew tulips for a living. The kitchen garden was a carpet of flaming red and orange tulips. Has ever a man appreciated the sight of tulips more than me that spring day?

Even more beautiful, my beloved children were waiting for me there, all dressed up and looking more grown up. Lidia, Vera, Daniel, and Anna lined up together with their grandma and granddad holding bundles of tulips. I hugged each of them and then we all hugged together in one big group embrace. Tears of joy rolled down our cheeks—the Bondarenko family was together again! Prison, with its backbreaking labor, bed bugs, lack of food, sleep, and fellowship . . . that was behind me now, and I could hopefully look forward to life as a husband, father, and minister of the gospel.

The table was set, and Anna, my mother-in-law, had prepared a feast. We gave extra thanks to God that day, for not just the delicious meal but for his loving-kindness in bringing me home.

I relished being back with my loved ones, in that cozy home, surrounded by my children who were eagerly interrupting each other to tell me three years' worth of news.

Lidia and Vera were so grown up, and they had been a big help to their mother and to their grandma with the cooking. They were smart and hardworking young ladies, and I was filled with pride for them.

Daniel had graduated from first grade and was excitedly telling me how he had learned to read and write.

Little Anna was four, and she never parted from her baby doll.

I was bursting with delight in them all, and in Maria, who acted as both mother and father for three years, raising four children with tenderness and discipline under great hardship. She taught our children to work hard and serve others, especially our numerous visitors, ministers, and believers of all kinds from all over, who came to share meals at our table.

Days flew by, and before I knew it came another day I had waited for with great anticipation: my reunion with my beloved church in Riga. It was incredibly moving to look out over my flock and see so many dear brothers and sisters who had prayed faithfully for me, sent me letters of encouragement, and supported my family while I was in prison.

Friends from Finland and Sweden as well as different republics of the Soviet Union came to share our joy, and many shared wishes and memories. We sang together and shared the Lord's Supper.

Truly, the joy was palpable. My presence among them as a free man was proof that God had answered their prayers and brought their pastor back where he belonged.

I was so emotional—I'm not ashamed to admit it. How could I ever thank these faithful friends who had never forgotten me while I was in prison, nor had ever forgotten my loved ones? I prayed that

God would pour out his blessings and gifts on each one of them, and repay them in a way I never could.

※ ※ ※

Latvia and the other Baltic countries had more freedom than some of the other Soviet countries. But even so, I never took my guard down in those still-dangerous years before the iron curtain fell.

There was a period of about five years where I had a bit more freedom to minister, but I was always aware that I was being watched and my church activities monitored. In my mind, this was a "calm before the storm," a period of unsettling quietness where the old rules still applied, even though I hadn't been arrested in quite a while.

In August 1986, that period ended. It was early in the morning and we had just returned from a trip to Belarus to visit family and friends.

We drove into the yard and left the car open with an ignition key in it. Daniel, my son, was about to take things out of the car when he saw militia men approaching the house. He was only a young boy, but he kept a cool head, ran for the door, and shut it in their faces.

Ten militia men banged on the door and demanded to be let in. One of them tried to get into the house through a window in the bathroom, but he couldn't get the window open as it was too small for him. "Let us in or we'll break your door down!" they threatened.

We had just precious few minutes to hide some books and documents and burn some letters. We finally let them in as they were about to pummel the door down. As they entered the house, the KGB conducted a careful search of all rooms, examining everything, every little piece of paper.

Our youngest child, Mariam, was just two (she was born almost two years after I got out of prison). She cried loudly at the chaos and intrusion caused by the rough men. The older children knew how to behave in such a situation. They were quiet and watchful for a way to help us.

We all knew there were some Christian books in the car, valuable resources to us and firewood for the KGB. How could we save them? Lidia had an idea. While the militia were rummaging through our house, she crept out to the car through the small window the militiaman had been unable to crawl through. The moment she knew for sure she wasn't being noticed Lidia grabbed the bag of books from the car and ran away to our neighbors' house through the vegetable garden.

Maria and I worried at times that the trauma of the persecutions and the constant monitoring of the KGB would affect our children's character and well-being. But God worked miracles in their hearts. They bravely withstood mocking at school and other hardships, and the Holy Spirit used it to strengthen their faith.

During the search, I noticed a KGB officer checking the books on a shelf. I watched as he slipped Aleksandr Solzhenitsyn's *The Gulag Archipelago* under his coat. This surprised me since the book was still underground and considered highly anti-Soviet. (*The Gulag Archipelago* has since become a classic as the best-known work about the Soviet forced labor camp system and Solzhenitsyn's own experiences as a prisoner in a Gulag labor camp. Written between 1958 and 1968, it was published in the West in 1973, thereafter circulating as an underground publication in the Soviet Union until its official publication in 1989.)

After the search, the KGB prepared to take me to a militia station with them. My children began to weep, begging them to not take me away. In the presence of militia we all fell to our knees and prayed. Of course, the militia had no patience for this. "Come on—stop praying right now! Your God won't help you." We stood up, and the children watched with tears in their eyes as I was led away.

I was brought to a militia station. After several hours of being detained, while they scrutinized documents and interrogated me, I was released. They didn't have enough evidence to detain me. I didn't know it at the time, but the KGB was searching the homes of my friends and church members that same day, combing their houses for evidence against me that would stick.

But nothing incriminating was found, at my house or any of the other houses. This time, I would not be locked up and separated from my loved ones. This time, God had other plans for me. Already, a crack had begun to form in the iron curtain, and soon everything would change.

22

Long-Expected Freedom

WHEN THE GODLESS REGIME finally collapsed, the atheists were shocked. How could this happen? How could their atheistic virtues and ideals not have worked to form the perfect society?

Having taken God out of the equation, they never expected Him to destroy their man-made stronghold, a steely grip that seemed unconquerable for so long. Those who "lifted up their heels against God" and His glory had disgraced themselves throughout the entire world. Christ prevailed, as he always will.

The prayers of Christians in every corner of the globe set in motion the greatest mercy: freedom, to live openly as believers and for all Christians everywhere to be able to share God's love and salvation with their neighbors. He used a political leader named Mikhail Gorbachev to start spinning the wheels of change.

Perestroika was a political movement for reformation within the Communist Party during the mid-1980s, widely associated with Gorbachev and his glasnost ("openness") policy reform. *Perestroika* means "restructuring" and refers to the shake-up of the Soviet political and economic system.

Under this new "openness," Gorbachev changed the meaning of freedom for the people of the Soviet Union. Previously, freedom had meant recognition of the atheist regime. Now, however, freedom meant escaping all constraints. Gorbachev ceased the persecution of religion, and the iron doors of prisons and work camps swung wide open.

By 1987, the freedoms our fathers had dreamed about, freedoms that thousands of believers had been praying for all over the world, came to pass. Those who came before us had died without seeing the unbelievable answer to their hopes and prayers, but we were honored to see it unfold in our time.

Unparalleled freedom was given to people in the former Soviet Union. Despite all the persecutions and repressions, the church in Russia had not only survived but thrived. We had freedom to preach the Good News, worship our God, and distribute that formerly embargoed weapon—the Bible. It was a dream come true for Christians all over the world who had prayed for this day to come. "You who have done great things; O God, who is like You?" (Ps. 71:19).

Our faithful compatriots who were living abroad were a part of a large family of those who were praying for us and participating in our sufferings. The famous Russian radio preacher Yarl Peisti wrote to believers in 1977:

> Not only grown-ups, but also children pray for you with tears in their eyes. They do so in Africa, the Near East, South and North America, in Asian countries, in Australia, New Zealand, and especially in European countries. We believe the Holy Spirit put this desire into the hearts of believers throughout the world. I see this as sign that God is preparing some special revival for your country.

So many Christian brothers and sisters worked tirelessly to help enact change for us behind the iron curtain.

German brothers Gerhard Hamm, Arnold Rose, Jakov Leven, and others sincerely and diligently worked in God's fields, fighting for freedom and the rights of believers of the Soviet Union.

Slavic brothers from the United States such as A. Garbuzyuk, P. Deineka, P. Rogozin, R. Berezov, and others did not forget about their countrymen but fought from their new home to defend persecuted believers in the Soviet Union.

P. Rogozin's books were like cold water for a Russian nation thirsting in a desert of atheism and godlessness. Nikolai Vodnevsky's articles, rich in spirit, and his poems, powerful in their simplicity and humanity, lit the way for believers suffering in a dark time. Poet Vera Kushnir's solicitation before the American government, and her poems, radio programs, and articles brought consolation and hope to believers.

My friend Romanian pastor Richard Wurmbrand was tortured for his faith and imprisoned for fourteen years, and afterwards devoted his whole life to helping persecuted Christians. He founded the Voice of the Martyrs, a ministry dedicated to assisting the persecuted church worldwide and finding ways to advocate for the rights and freedoms of such believers. "Remember the prisoners, as though in prison with them, and those who are ill-treated, since you yourselves also are in the body" (Heb. 13:3). The shining lives and self-sacrificing ministry of Richard and his wife, Sabina, are known to Christians throughout the world.

As a result of numerous solicitations of Christian organizations and advocates like these before the US Congress and Senate, a quota was issued for believing immigrants from the USSR, and as a result eight hundred thousand Christians from the Soviet Union immigrated to the United States.

Another page of Russian history was turning over, and a new and longed-for liberty came to us.

The Bible says, "The people who walk in darkness will see a great light" (Isa. 9:2), and that's exactly what happened. During President Gorbachev's era, there were vast changes, not only in the political life of the country, but in freedom of faith for Christians.

On the president's personal instruction, believers of all confessions and prisoners of conscience were released from prisons. The Cold War was over, and God was using Gorbachev in His plan to destroy false Communist ideas, whether or not the president was aware of his part in that plan or not. "The king's heart is like channels of water in the hand of the LORD; He turns it wherever He wishes" (Prov. 21:1).

My family and I were privileged to meet Gorbachev and we will never forget it. We met the great man in 2000, at a dinner given in honor of the tenth anniversary of the fall of Berlin Wall, held at the German Society Club in Anahaim, California.

It was an unforgettable and historic event for us all. Who would have thought things would change to such an extent in our country? My dream to personally testify to Mr. Gorbachev about the Lord came true. I told him about my family, and that we were praying for him and his family, and also thanked him for the changes he had enacted for believers in the former Soviet Union. Gorbachev listened attentively and remarked that it was good that we had moved to the United States. I wished him success and blessings, and we parted.

Truly, God's ways are inscrutable. He used a great man, though an unbeliever, to bring about His purposes. We pray that Mikhail Gorbachev will one day make changes in his own heart and soul, and that he would find peace with the God who used him so greatly.

Significant credit also goes to some world leaders, including several American presidents. We are deeply grateful to George H. W. Bush, Ronald Reagan, Jimmy Carter, and Bill Clinton for their advocacy for the freedom and rights of believers and people of conscience. From places of power, they helped us achieve autonomy and greater liberty. And countless ordinary people and many faithful believers in the United states did what they could to help us as well, and we will never forget that as long as we live.

23

A Church in Riga

MY MINISTRY AS A PASTOR in Riga flourished with the new freedoms, and God's vineyard yielded a bountiful harvest.

The history of the Cross Baptist Church in Latvia is rich and inimitable. To describe it in the detail it deserves would take another book. I started this church with a few families, and with God's blessing it grew to be the largest Baptist church in Riga.

As mentioned earlier Latvia has a different culture, distinct from other republics of the USSR. Our church consisted of new believers and people who had come from all parts of the Soviet Union. Under the new freedoms, it was an incredible experience to build our church, filled with dynamic young people and progressive, innovative programs.

We held literature evenings, and musical and spiritually educative services. These services were so exciting and unusual that young believers from Estonia, Lithuania, and other republics used to visit our church to watch, listen, and learn. Our young people loved new ideas and willingly put them into practice in various projects and ministry efforts.

People were coming to the Lord in droves, and these new believers brought a vigor and spark to our body of believers. Church members of all ages encouraged each other to work eagerly and to pray.

As a church we had tremendous unity, as we strove to be one in Christ. As people who had lost so much in the past—homes, loved ones, and freedoms—we worked together to build each other up in the truth. God blessed our unity with miracles, healings, and opened the doors wide for those outside the church to look at us and be drawn to Him. My priority was to share with young people my testimony of God's grace and rescue. I wanted to inspire them to grow and become spiritually mature. Our young believers used to visit other churches and hold services and meetings there. No one wanted to miss those trips. Such experiences bonded the young people together and gave them confidence about their strength and possibilities in the Lord.

It's also been my privilege to mentor and grow new church leaders. I have a passion for the new generation to learn and be trained in the service of the Lord. I have always loved to bring up new leaders and give them opportunities to grow into their potential.

The sky was now the limit, and we pushed as far as possible to spread the Word, taking evangelistic trips to vast expanses of Siberia—from Riga to Novosibirsk and Irkutsk. We partnered with churches in Moldova as well as in Bryansk, Russia and all over Russia to preach the Good News.

We never stood still. During these years, it often felt like we were living in the early church in times of the apostles. We supported each other in worldly and spiritual needs. We loved one another through thick and thin. We grew together in truth and grace. It would truly take another book to list all the stories and all the joys and blessings from my time as pastor of the church in Riga. The story of our lives together as one church body is unique, and I'm so grateful God allowed me to be part of that story.

An Evangelistic Meeting in Estonia

The year 1988 was declared the one-thousand-year anniversary of the baptism of Russia, celebrated both by Orthodox believers and Protestants. With the new freedoms, this was a fantastic occasion to preach the gospel in widespread ways never before experienced in the twentieth century. Large-scale evangelistic meetings were held in the most prestigious stadiums and houses of culture around the country. We were finally allowed to preach openly, and the anniversary gave us the perfect chance to do so.

The first big crusade took place in Tallinn, Estonia. Earlier in the year, I had been approached by Estonian brothers who traveled to Riga and asked me to lead a crusade in a massive sports palace named after Vladimir Lenin. I loved their enthusiasm and initiative, and joyfully accepted their proposal.

But to be honest, I was concerned: how would we hold a service for ten thousand people? We had never held services of that magnitude before. When I told my church about the idea, everyone was very excited and determined to make it work. We made up our minds to fast and pray.

I invited evangelist Victor Hamm from Canada, popular Christian singer Victor Klimenko from Finland, and young opera soloist and conductor Peter Kravchuk to participate in the crusade and organize a mass choir. Choir singers from a "revival" church of Riga, a choir from a Russian church in Tallinn, and our church sang together and took an active part in the service.

On the appointed day, we arrived in Tallinn, having coordinated the crusade with local believers and our own church members. We came to the center of the town, where the V. I. Lenin Palace of Sports and Culture (now called Linnahall) was situated, and were struck speechless. We couldn't believe our eyes: there were tons of people streaming into the Palace!

We found out later that news of the Tallinn crusade had reached dozens of churches throughout the Soviet Union. Believers traveled from all corners on trains, planes, and automobiles. The seating capacity of the venue was ten thousand, and clearly it soon would not be able to accommodate everyone. The place was overfilled. What could we do?

Someone had the idea that the ice fields next to the venue could be covered in wooden panels and chairs. The managers of the Palace kindly agreed with the suggestion, and a few thousand people filled the ice fields quickly.

Both Russians and Estonians sat side by side, so Estonian pastor Arpad Arder and I prayed in two languages, thus opening the service. The stadium was filled with the music of the mass choir, and a wave of the Holy Spirit swept over us. A sense of reverence could be felt in every corner. Something extraordinary was taking place, a fact later evidenced by the throngs of people not walking, but running forward to repent of their sins, without any fear. That day hundreds of people received new life and peace with God.

The crusade in Tallinn gave impetus to planning more evangelistic crusades in many cities of the Soviet Union. A mass baptism service was held on the Dnieper River in Kiev, Ukraine, and crusades followed in Kursk, Russia, then in Brest, Belarus, Bryansk, Russia, Chernovtsy and Odessa, Ukraine, Kishinev, Moldova, and other cities.

An Evangelistic Meeting in Uzbekistan

Just before a planned crusade in Tashkent, Uzbekistan, in May 1988, however, I had another heart attack. An ambulance took me to a hospital where I was being prepped for open heart surgery. My heart attack came as no surprise. Nine years of living in prison conditions had undermined my health. Maria and I were told the operation was inevitable.

I was depressed and frustrated by this turn of events. Here I was, finally free to preach and do all the things I had been forbidden to do for so long, and now I was stuck in a hospital bed! I had a lot of time to think and pray, and one night it came to me what I should do. I scooted down off my bed, fell to my knees and prayed: "Lord,

I *have* to go to Tashkent. If You still need me here on the earth, restore me!"

After the prayer, I felt better immediately. I got up and realized God had regarded me with favor. He healed me! He performed a miracle! I couldn't sleep anymore and all night long I thanked him for his wonderful healing power.

In the morning, I refused to be operated on and signed a document stating that the doctors were no longer responsible for my health and life. I was discharged from the Pauls Stradins Clinical University Hospital in Riga, and two days later left for Tashkent with my wife. There, in a house of prayer on 35 Panchenko Street, I preached at a beautiful, multinational celebration of Russians and Uzbeks. The Holy Spirit and the word of God's grace touched many lives, and people turned their lives over to the God who had healed me.

24

Revival

REVIVAL EMBRACED THE ENTIRE COUNTRY. God urged me to act boldly, with no hesitation, and I in turn urged believers all over the country to join the evangelism movement and share their faith. Acting in this spirit of boldness, I invited well-known Christian speakers and evangelists from the West to come and speak. Among them were the American astronauts James Irwin and Charles Duke, and evangelists Luis Palau, Yarl Peisti, Victor Hamm, Richard Wurmbrand, and Arnold Rose.

Mass evangelistic crusades took place in parks, palaces of culture, and stadiums in Moscow Leningrad (now Saint Petersburg), Safonovo, Russia; Kishinev, Moldova; Zakarpatye, Ukraine; and Jurmala, Latvia. In our beloved Riga we held a meeting in an arena that held thirty thousand people.

We couldn't have orchestrated these wonderful crusades without the help of my son-in-law, Peter Kravchuk, the talented singer and conductor and Latvian State Conservatory graduate whom I mentioned earlier. Peter's priceless contribution of managing the musical programs for these services was a source of great inspiration and blessing for the listeners.

Yarl Peisti, my friend, was also a much-loved evangelist and Christian broadcast minister known to millions of Russians. Here are some of his memories of the times we partnered in ministry:

My dear friend and Christian brother Joseph,

Our first meeting in Kiev in 1988 was a starting point in a chain of our many meetings. We had been familiar with one another for many years before meeting. We wrote letters to one another, and I did my best to support prisoners, including you, through my radio programs.

Because of you, I had the chance to visit a Soviet prison. Do you remember that day? It was you, me, and the astronaut Charles Duke, being driven to the prison in Tsesis, Latvia, in a black government automobile to hold a gathering in the prison.

There was a militia escort driving in front of us, and we were followed by a few dozen Zhigulis [Ladas], driven by young people from your church. My wife, Pirkko, was with them. We approached the prison. We saw huge iron gates opened. We were met by a major, the chief warden, who greeted us in a friendly way and gave some short remarks. To me, that day was a dream come true, the first time I could testify for prisoners personally, not through the radio.

Joseph, do you remember our ministry in Zakarpatye, Ukraine? There was a big tent set up in the very center of the town. The construction looked like a huge greenhouse. There was in fact a kind of greenhouse effect inside the tent, which became stuffy fast. Some local brothers punctured holes in the roof of the tent to let some fresh air in. After the sermon, people began to come forward to give their lives to the Lord. Under their weight, the platform began to sink down and slowly press itself into the ground. "The Lord will meet you there where you are now," we called out. "Stay in your seats!"

That service in Brest, Belarus, was interesting, too. Some extraordinary things were happening. One of the big church buildings of the independent congregation on Fortechnaya Street could not accommodate all the visitors. The service took place in a parking lot near the house of prayer, and a central stairway served as a platform and a pulpit for speakers. I don't remember for sure how many thousands of people came. I remember you and me, together with the local brothers, were standing on the top of the stairs, and the choir members were standing on lower ones. Everyone stood on their feet for three hours in the burning sun, but the crowd was quite patient. Some of them climbed up the roof of a building next door, and some climbed trees. It was unforgettable.

It was my great desire to visit your church in Riga, as I had heard so much about it. That Sunday, you were having visitors from Sweden and a brass band was playing. You moved everybody to the churchyard and people from neighboring streets began to come, attracted by the sounds of the brass band. That was my first time in the Baltic region. What a joy it was to see my radio listeners face to face, to talk to them one on one. So many people were crying; there were deep emotions at that service.

One trip surpassed all our expectations: our meeting in the Philippines. The Lausanne Congress was taking place there, and more than three thousand Christians came from all over the world.

For the first time in the history of the Soviet Union, a Russian delegation was given permission to leave the country and go abroad. The delegation consisted of approximately sixty ministers. The Congress committee had not expected our Russian delegation to arrive on time because of all the bureaucracy, so we were not included in the official program. When the chairman of the Congress, Leighton Ford, was informed of our arrival, he told us we could only have ten minutes to speak, five for the speaker and five for the interpreter. This was a firm time limit.

So, the question became who should be chosen to speak on behalf of the Russian brothers? And you, Joseph, were chosen.

You immediately drew the attention of the entire hall. Stillness fell over the crowd as delegates hung on your every word. You spoke of how the church had survived in Stalin's Gulags and camps of death, defending the purity of the gospel. You were talking for half an hour instead of ten minutes. When you were done, the crowd gave you a standing ovation. They were inspired by this living witness, who had gone through prisons, camps, and the hell of Communist cruelty and had remained faithful to Christ. Everybody took their seats. We saw Leighton Ford coming towards us, and we thought he was going to say something about you going over the time limit. But instead he said, "Why did you stop speaking?"

There were so many blessings for us, working together in the fields God had prepared for us, witnessing together in the former Soviet Union! Those times were just the beginning. I believe that before Christ's return, many more people in Russia will enter God's kingdom.

With love, your friend and brother in Christ,

Yarl Peisti

From the start, God gifted me with courage, enthusiasm, and the desire to take risks for Him. I always had big ideas for the kingdom and God, and He helped me bring them to life, despite the skepticism of many.

New Opportunities

In the very beginning of perestroika ("restructuring"), we organized a church mission called Evangelism and Works of Mercy. It was formed to help people spiritually and materially. We gave out New Testaments, Bibles, and showed the *JESUS* film in whatever language the people spoke. We visited the sick and the elderly in retirement homes. Missionary groups worked in schools, institutes, and prisons. Young believers joyfully participated in local and international expeditions, gaining the golden experience of missionary work.

In 1991, God put the desire in my heart to organize a missionary trip to Siberia. I wanted to bring the Good News of salvation to people living in those very places where our Christian brothers and sisters had suffered terribly for their faithfulness.

We started planning for the trip, but right before we were about to go the devil threw up a huge obstacle: the 1991 Soviet coup d'état, also known as the August Putsch or August Coup. This was an attempt by a group of hard-line members of the Communist Party to take control of the country from President Mikhail Gorbachev. They were opposed to Gorbachev's reform program and the new union treaty he had negotiated that decentralized much of the Soviet Union government's power to the republics.

Everybody was shocked and worried. What would happen next? Maria and I were in Switzerland at the time and had just gotten off the phone (a terrible, broken connection) with our daughter Lidia, who begged us not to come home to Latvia. "Daddy, as soon as you return, you will be imprisoned!"

Authorities in Switzerland immediately proposed political asylum for us and issued a residential permit for us to live in their country. We joined the entire world in anxiously watching what would happen in our country. Would the USSR revert to totalitarianism? For seventy years, our people had been choked by the Soviet regime, and we were crushed at the thought of returning to an atheist state.

Two days later, though, the situation brought about a dramatic turning point: the coup collapsed after a short but effective campaign of civil resistance, and Gorbachev returned to power. The coup ended up weakening and damaging the Soviet Union and is widely considered to have contributed to both the demise of the Communist Party and the dissolution of the Soviet Union.

And our trip to Siberia took place, as planned.

We had chills down our spines as we flew to Siberia for the first time ever on a flight chartered by believers, 150 of us joining together in a mission called Christ for the People of Siberia. Considering what had nearly just happened with the coup, we relished our freedoms all the more and everyone was deeply affected by the significance of the flight.

From Tobolsk, Siberia, we boarded the ship *TOBOL* and sailed to different ports along the rivers Irtysh and Ob, preaching in many towns and villages where God's message had never been proclaimed.

Then we undertook four expeditions to Western Siberia, from Tyumen to the Yamal Peninsula. (In Nenets, the language of the region, *Yamal* means "the end of the world.") My assistant, evangelist Leonid Pastukhov, took an active part in organizing the trips and I am grateful for his help. We brought the gospel news to prisons and camps, juvenile correctional facilities, hospitals, educational institutions and orphanages, and also military facilities.

There in forsaken Siberia, where our Christian brothers had for many years sown the seeds of truth and watered them with their tears, we reaped the harvest with joy. At one of baptismal services in Siberia, a former militia man gave me his photo, and on the back he wrote the following:

From your former persecutor, yet now a brother in Christ whom you baptized today, in the name of the Lord Jesus Christ.

Respectfully, Brother Valery, baptized by you, Joseph, July 7, 1993 in Khanty-Mansiysk.

More than ten new churches were planted in Siberia during that trip, and to this very day our missionary brothers and sisters are working diligently there.

One of the plants was an Evangelical church in the town of Salekhard, the only town in the world with suburbs north of the polar circle. The town was often used as a place of exile during the Soviet period and contained three Soviet camps where approximately 6,500 prisoners were held, who were arrested for their belief in God. At the town's port, around 1,500 prisoners loaded and unloaded goods at the dock or mined metal ores. About 5,000 prisoners in the two other camps were assigned to polish diamonds mined from Mirny.

A new church building was built on precisely the same site where once stood an office of Stalin's Gulag. Thousands of brothers and sisters went through its torture chambers, never to return to their families. Would they ever have believed that one day a church would stand in the place of their torture and death? God is so good! My astronaut friend Charles Duke joined me on one of these trips to Siberia as did his dear wife, Dotty, on two other occasions elsewhere. Here are his recollections of the ministry the Lord allowed us to share together:

> As the Cold War was winding down in 1989, I received an invitation from Joseph Bondarenko to come to Russia and Latvia to share my faith in Jesus. I flew to Moscow and then boarded a train for Riga, Latvia, where I was met by a band and the congregation of Joseph's church. When I stepped off the train, I saw this man who glowed with the love of Jesus. It was Joseph. That meeting started a ministry together that took us all over Latvia, Lithuania, Eastern Russia, and eventually to Siberia. Everywhere we went, Joseph's preaching was electrifying and many came to faith in Christ.

> With my wife, Dotty, I made two more trips to Russia to speak at various venues that Joseph had organized. Everywhere we spoke, the Lord confirmed His Word and many came to know Jesus. Once we met in the offices of the KGB, where Joseph shared his story of arrests and persecutions at their hands. In a very moving moment, Joseph said he had forgiven them and there was healing and prayer between old enemies.

> Our trip to Siberia was empowered by the Holy Spirit as we traveled from place to place. Joseph's preaching was anointed and many came to faith. We visited churches that Joseph had helped plant and, like the apostle Paul, he encouraged the believers.

> I have met few men with the passion for God and the zeal for evangelism that Joseph possesses. He has been an influential mentor for me and my wife. His zeal is infectious. I praise God for bringing Joseph and his family into my life. May his

testimony and story inspire many to give their all for Jesus, just as Joseph has done.

In July 1992, about a thousand delegates, ministering brothers from all the regions of the country and also many countries of the West, came together in Riga to participate in a conference called Nations for Christ. The aim of the conference was to bring together all our efforts to bring the Good News to all the regions of our multinational country. The conference greatly encouraged the delegates and fueled the fires of missions in Russia.

An article was published about the conference in the Riga newspaper, written by journalist Inna Kanevskaya. She wrote: "Now all the sufferings are behind, and Joseph Bondarenko, a pastor of the "Cross" church, a father of five children, can freely preach Christ's teaching everywhere . . . He enjoys the right to go abroad, to come to editorial offices of Soviet newspapers, [and] to hold conferences."

One of the attendees wrote me a letter afterwards:

Dear Joseph,

I read an article about you in our newspaper for young people, and I learned about the persecutions you faced for the sake of your faith. The conference made an indelible impression on me and forced me to reexamine some of my views. Many of the troubles in our society are not only the result of a confusing and unworkable economic system, but also of its seventy-year-long era of having a soulless, meaningless existence. For so long, we lost our ideals and faith, and consequently our moral values. I praise God that those in power finally began to realize that *prohibiting the natural conversation between God and the nation is a senseless crime.*

The letter writer was absolutely correct: the Soviet system tried to suppress what is natural and inborn in every human heart—the desire to know the God who created them. It was a seventy-year exercise in futility, and God brought glory to himself by toppling the regime that said He didn't exist.

Historic Days in Moscow

In 1992, I was invited to be part of the organizing committee for a major evangelistic effort called Revival, and our job was to prepare for a crusade with Billy Graham in Moscow.

I had the opportunity to be part of many pre-crusade gatherings as well as many meetings with Russian government officials. That summer brought amazing, historic events that astounded me as I witnessed how far we had come.

On one occasion alluded to above, I, along with astronaut Charles Duke and other members of our Revival committee, prayed for state officials in the building of the KGB office on Lubyanka Street. We poured out our hearts to God in the very same room that once belonged to Felix Dzerzhinsky, one of the infamous heroes of the October Revolution of 1917.

During the reception at those offices, a vice chairman of the Soviet Union's KGB stood up in front of all present and asked forgiveness for all the prison terms my Christian brothers and I once received on their orders. "We know how much you have suffered," he said. "From now on, things will be different." Silence enveloped the room. It was a one-of-a-kind moment.

The interpreter translated the words of the KGB general for foreign delegates, and everybody stood up. "As God forgave me, I forgive you," I told the KGB vice chairman. I thanked him for his sincerity and asked him to announce his confession to the media. Then, after many months of laying the groundwork, the Billy Graham crusade took place, in the world capital of atheism, not far from the walls of the Kremlin. It was the greatest of miracles. For three days, forty-five thousand people burst at the seams of the Olympic Stadium and spilled over into the parking lots, where huge video screens broadcast Graham's message.

This was a genuine celebration for the people of God, and it reminded me of the Bible's account of the days of Solomon's coronation: "The people were playing on flutes and rejoicing with great joy, so that the earth shook at their noise" (1 Kings 1:40).

A Tajik woman, Shirinai Dosova, gave a mighty testimony, as

did Joni Eareckson Tada and many others. There were masses of people, yet everyone listened with bated breath at their stories of lives changed by God.

It was stunning to behold the orchestra of the Soviet Armed Forces, holding the Order of the Red Banner, as Russian soldiers and officers sang in bold voices "Glory, glory, hallelujah!" A mass choir of seven thousand singers from Evangelical churches in the Soviet Union opened the service with Mozart's praise anthem. My son-in-law Peter Kravchuk was one of three conductors (A. Kreshchuk and V. Kreiman were the others).

There had never been such a celebration and triumph of believers. Each service ended with Dr. Graham's altar call and the singing of the hymn "Just as I Am." The Holy Spirit tenderly touched people's hearts and thousands of people flowed forward to pledge their hearts to Jesus Christ.

Doctors, engineers, teachers, students, military men, militia men, representatives of committees on religious affairs, and former KGB members were coming to God. One of them, Semen Osadchuk, a colonel in the Ministry of Internal Affairs, believed and was baptized with his entire family. As a KGB officer, he had been present at my first trial in Odessa in 1962. How rewarding it was for me to witness his transformation! He was a dear guest in our home and in our church many times.

A lot of beautiful souls were added to our churches—only God knows how many.

Churches that had been destroyed and closed were being restored and repaired. New church buildings were being raised up before our eyes. The Traxel family gave generous financial support so that prayer houses could be built in Siberia, Latvia, Ukraine, Russia, and Crimea.

Our fathers and mothers, brothers and sisters, who gave their lives for their Lord, were not allowed to see the fruit of their sacrifices, but I know God richly rewarded them in heaven.

I was not only honored to see the changes with my own eyes, but to bring my testimony of God's grace to many countries around the world. The Lord gave me opportunities to tell about His omnipotence in America, Canada, Australia, Japan, Israel, Germany, France, England, Switzerland, Holland, Sweden, Korea, Philippines, Denmark, Norway, Finland, Poland, and Tasmania. Sometimes when I would visit those places, I would think about the times that KGB officers would sneer at me, promising me that neither I nor my children would ever escape the Soviet Union. But God has demonstrated over and over that faith and truth always win in the end.

I recall that in 1978, I refused the invitation of three countries—Canada, the United States, and Australia—to gain asylum away from my homeland. I don't regret it, even though I ended up going to prison again for three years after that. Because had I left Russia, I never would have experienced the vast blessings and triumphs of ten years of perestroika, working alongside my family to bring truth and grace to our fellow countrymen.

In 1998, God resettled us in America. I became a pastor of a newly formed Slavic Evangelical Missionary Church in Orange County, California. When I retired as senior pastor of the church, I founded the Good Call Ministries, a nonprofit organization that continues to support churches in Siberia and minister to the local communities throughout the United States.

I am so grateful to God for all that He has allowed me to do for Him. However, when we look back on our lives, it's not important what *we* do, but what *God* is doing, constantly going ahead of us and achieving His purposes. He invites each one of us to be co-workers with the Lord Jesus Christ in building up His church and praying for His kingdom to come on the earth as it is in heaven. He doesn't want our success. He wants nothing more than our whole hearts. "Great and marvelous are Your works, O Lord God, the Almighty; Righteous and true are Your ways, King of the nations!" (Rev. 15:3).

Epilogue

A Visit to My Old Prison

I DIDN'T KNOW IT on that sunny day in May 1981, when I was released from prison for what would be the last time, but God was already sowing seeds of change in people's hearts all over Russia.

It was during perestroika that I visited my old prison in Tlyustenhabl near Krasnodar accompanied by my friend, Apollo 16 astronaut Charles Duke and his wife, Dotty. From what has already been said about Charlie, some in his own words, it was no surprise that Charlie and Dotty became dear and lifelong friends. I haven't met another man yet who's as accomplished as Charlie is, yet also so approachable, simple, and humble. He was a vital part of my ministry in Russia and the United States, and God used him tremendously to bring the Good News to the most intellectual and educated people in Russia.

I will never forget the visit we made to my old prison that day as long as I live. We entered the barrack I lived in before my third discharge; it was my last prison cell. Charles and Dotty placed thirty roses on my bunk bed, ten for each year I had been in that prison. On their faces I could see fear, surprise, and admiration that I had endured living in such conditions.

In that horrible place, where men's hearts and lives were broken into pieces, we tearfully prayed, for current and past inmates and for their jailers. The guards and prison officials accompanying us were shocked that we would become so emotional. They took off their uniform caps, and stood in silence, listening to us pray and watching us pour out our hearts.

Following that time in my old cell, all the prisoners gathered to hear Charles speak about his moon flight, and about God, the Creator of all things visible and invisible. On my request, even those in solitary confinement were brought to hear Charles, even though in the beginning the camp authorities had been resistant. I promised them that they would each receive a Bible with the famous astronaut's autograph. That seemed to do the trick and they quite quickly agreed.

I was deeply affected by the experience of returning to my prison home, and to witness God's grace poured out on those prisoners, who were living through some of the same darkness and despair I had once been subjected to. It was a wonder of wonders. To have been told that my faith would always be held in contempt by the prison officials and by members of the Soviet society, and then to be allowed to share that faith in those dingy, airless walls—Wow! God is good, all the time. All the time, God is good.

In Retrospect

I'VE BEEN LUCKY TO BE a small particle in the great history of Christians, to have lived and worked in the company of faithful and blessed people. I've tried to imitate their faith, their patience, and their courage.

In these pages, I've tried to describe my experiences and those of the men and women I've walked alongside, working together in God's fields. I haven't attempted to evaluate meaning and significance the movements and events through which we have lived. I'll leave that to the historians.

Herein these memoirs, I have offered my joys, victories, mistakes, grief and disappointments, and my account of how the Lord's strong hands upheld me and made me stand firm. Despite some intolerable conditions and attacks on me by strangers and my own people alike, the Lord helped me preserve the dignity of my heavenly title. Through deprivations filtered through His own hand, I taught myself to rely upon the Lord alone.

"The testimony of our conscience, that in holiness and godly sincerity, not in fleshly wisdom but in the grace of God, we have conducted ourselves in the world" (2 Cor. 1:12). This is the essence of my life and my mission.

Prison was for me God's university, a master class in humility and the act of loving one's enemies. Gold is tested by fire, and a man by sufferings. My bondage became the greatest academy, where my heart was melted, tested, and sanctified for further ministry.

In seminary, a pastor is taught theory, and in prison, one is taught practice. My faith, my love, and my faithfulness were tested repeatedly. Yet God gave me strength to proclaim the Good News of salvation for the perishing world.

My generation has been lucky enough to see three historic periods: the era of our fathers and mothers, who endured the unendurable yet managed to preserve their faith; our own battle with atheism; and, finally, the period of beloved freedom to preach the gospel and pass the torch to the next generation.

Maria and I count it one of our greatest joys that our five children love the Lord and serve Him. The Lord gave our family great mutual respect for each other and strong friendship. During many years our kids shared in the hardships and blessings of the ministry. God allowed me to baptize all of my children and bless their marriages.

Truly, I can't overestimate my family's assistance in writing this book. I want to express my particular gratitude to my wife, Maria—my helper in all things, and my daughter Vera, who carefully read my notes and corrected my mistakes. Without them and my other children, this book scarcely would have been written.

Finally, I want to thank all of my friends, who supported me with their letters and prayers, blessing me and encouraging me to finish the book. My deepest gratitude is for the One, Who gave me strength to endure all trials: "I am unworthy of all the lovingkindness and of all the faithfulness which You have shown to Your servant" (Gen. 32:10).

To my children, my grandchildren, and all the young generation who will be living in the twenty-first century, I pass to you the baton of pure faith and the preaching of the Good News. Wear with dignity for your whole lives the grace you have been given.

May God help you to find the right course, to design the best itinerary for your life in the Lord. Whatever things change in the world and in society—the gospel, as well as Christ and His Great Commission, never change.

Years ago, when I was going through my trials, the Lord spoke to me, telling me that one day in the future I would understand His purposes. Like Joseph, the son of Jacob, I came to know the truth of these words: "You meant evil against me, but God meant it for good in order to bring about this present result" (Gen. 50:20).

About the Author
and The Good Call Ministries

JOSEPH BONDARENKO (ThD, International Theological Seminary) is beloved in his native Russia and around the world as a pastor, an evangelist, and the organizer of countless crusades. He is known as the "Billy Graham of Russia."

Joseph was born and grew up in Ukraine. He attended the Naval Academy but was expelled because of his faith just before graduation. He was condemned to prison three times, serving a total of nearly ten years of imprisonment for preaching God's Word.

He is married and has five children and six granddaughters. All his children are Christian believers and serve the Lord. Joseph now wlives and ministers in Southern California with his family.

THE GOOD CALL MINISTRIES is a Christian non-profit organization based in California that was founded by Joseph Bondarenko. It serves the needs of local communities and Bible-based churches internationally, equipping the saints for the work of the Lord, providing training for prospective Christian leaders, assisting with youth seminars and guest speakers, and reaching out to the unsaved with the Good News. TGCM also supports newly-established Christian churches, orphanages, and missionaries in Ukraine and Russia.

The Good Call Ministries
PO Box 4694
Mission Viejo, CA 92690
Phone: 949.309.4549
E-mail: info@goodcallministries.org
Website: goodcallministries.org